A Friendly Dialogue

Between an

Atheist

and a

Christian

This is a dialogue between an atheist and the theist
Between a scientist and a Christian evangelist
Between one from the East and one from the West

Contents

Part one On the Bible and God   7

Part two On the Creation   19

Part three On Religion and the Spirit   27

Part four On Religious Beliefs in China   49

Part five On Chinese and Western Cultures and Philosophy   61

Part six On Religion and Science   79

Part seven On Religion and Social Harmony   111

Acknowledgments

By Luis Palau
& Zhao Qizheng

It is a tremendously complicated and difficult task to translate the manuscripts, communicate between the two authors and make publishing arrangements for this book, due to its unique theme and simultaneous publishing of both the Chinese and English editions. Without the strong support from many Chinese and American friends, this book could not have been published in time. We wish to extend sincere thanks to Mr. Lin Wusun and his wife Madame Zhang Qingnian for translating and proof-reading the manuscripts. They watched the video tape of the dialogues time and again, and their translation matches the original style of the conversations between the two authors, which is a rare achievement. We thank Mr. Zhang Hongbin for interpreting for and communicating between the two authors; Dr. Yao Junmei for bringing the notes of the dialogues, running to 70,000 words, to a concise text as it reads today; Mr. Yan Kejia, Director of the Institute of Religious Studies, Shanghai Academy of Social Sciences and Mr. Zhuo Xinping, Director of the Institute of World Religious Studies, Chinese Academy of Social Sciences, for their guidance in ensuring the accuracy of the religious terms; Madame Wu Wei for consulting with American friends on publishing affairs; Mr. Jay Fordice for his editing work with the English version; Mr. Bob Arnold, who was an invaluable liaison among the parties; Mr. Rob Tucker, Mr. David Wright and everyone at ZDL for their hard work; Dr. Enoch Wan for his insights; Jim and Jan Bisenius for their gift of hospitality extended to our friends from China; Mr. Chen Shilin, Mr. Brad Persons and other photographers for providing the photos. We thank the Information Offices of the State Council and Shanghai Municipal Government for providing excellent logistic support for the dialogues.

We thank Mr. Huang Youyi, Vice-President of the Federation of International Translators and Vice-Chairman and Secretary-General of the Translators Association of China, for his generous attention to the translation and editing of the book.

We should also thank Mr. Paul Chui for serving as interpreter for the dialogue and Dr. Lai Shenghan for communicating tirelessly between the two authors.

Last but not least, we should thank Mr. Chen Zuming and Mr. Shi Lei of the China Association for International Friendly Contact for facilitating the dialogues.

Prologue

By Luis Palau

Ever since I was a young boy growing up in Argentina, I have heard stories about the amazing country of China. I have dreamed about China, its people, its history and its culture. I love China. I want the best for this great nation and everyone within its borders. And now, after getting better acquainted with such a wonderful leader as Mr. Zhao Qizheng, my love and respect for China has only grown greater.

I believe with my whole heart that God loves China. I believe he has a special message for China and wants nothing more than to share his love with the entire nation.

It is for this reason that I felt so honored to be the invited guest of Mr. Zhao Qizheng, a gracious and respectable man I now have the privilege of calling my friend. I have been blessed by our conversations over the last year, speaking openly and honestly about our beliefs, understandings and misconceptions about each other's culture. I believe that as a result, we both have gained new understanding.

As Mr. Zhao so eloquently declared, our views on God, the world and eternity differ in many ways. But as we have also shown, that has not kept us from growing into true friends-individuals who mutually respect each other. As a Christian evangelist, I believe whole-heartedly in the Bible—God's Word—and its relevance and power to transform our lives.

It is my privilege and responsibility to introduce Jesus Christ, his teachings and his gift of eternal life, to the world. It is a calling I hold dearly, for I believe Jesus Christ offers tremendous power, freedom and eternal satisfaction to both nations and individuals.

It is Mr. Zhao's role as a highly accomplished and respected scientist to weigh matters based on logic, facts, formulas and proven findings. As a result, this conversation between the two of us has been lively, honest and thought-provoking. We have freely used our own areas of expertise to better understand our world and our reason for existence. I hope you find our dialogue to be just as intriguing as we did.

I hope that as our conversations progress, we will continue to build a bridge between our two societies. That our open and honest dialogue will lead to further understanding of the truth, while at the same time fostering respect and love and true friendship for one another, despite our deep differences.

Thank you for letting me come to you, reveal my heart, gain new friends and see first-hand the country I have prayed for over the past seventy years. I love China. ▪

Zhao Qizheng and Luis Palau at the news conference after the talks on Nov. 17, 2005

Dr. Palau said, "We came at it from the points of view of an atheist and a believer, but we soon realized that we have a lot in common as human beings, that we respect each other and we enjoy each other's company. I am truly impressed by Mr. Zhao's knowledge of not only science and philosophy, but also culture, international relations and theology. He elicited from me things I haven't thought about in 30 years. We are going to publish our conversations in English and I hope the book will help Americans understand the mindset of a thinking person in China, his enthusiasm for knowledge and the amazing changes taking place in China."

Mr. Zhao Qizheng said at the same press conference, "Dr. Palau and I are both rather pure species of our two different cultures. Because both of us were very straightforward during our discussions, we were able to breach the barriers posed by different ideologies and exchange views on a wide range of topics. It also set me thinking about many issues which I was originally not so familiar with. I was deeply touched when Dr. Palau told me he loved China. And because we were sincere and honest, the differences of beliefs did not constitute a barrier between us, neither did the difference in language or educational background. It is clear that our common objective is to promote global harmony."

Zhao and Palau having a picture taken after the talks

May 20, 2005,
At the reception room of the State Council Information Office,
Beijing, China.

Zhao Qizheng giving a speech at the 2005 Beijing *Fortune Global Forum*

Palau: Well, Mr. Zhao. The major media have written a lot about you. Having co—sponsored the *Fortune* Global Forum recently, you have become a front—paged figure in the papers. I have seen you covered in the press and by the TV stations. I know you are very busy and I am greatly honored to be here today. When I talked to my wife on the phone, I told her I was going to meet with the Mr. Zhao she saw on the TV, she said, "Why not take me along? I want to see him too."

Zhao: Well, she is welcome to come to China. It is too bad that we don't have a TV crew here or else she would be able to see us.

Palau: I regret I didn't bring her along. It would be very nice if we had our meeting televised.

Zhao Qizheng answering questions posed by Chinese and foreign journalists

Zhao: I have two friends in the American religious circles: Mr. Paul Crouch, President of TBN, and Mr. Marion Gordon "Pat" Robertson, Chairman of CBN.

Palau: They are my friends too. Mr. Crouch sent his regards. He told me he had once given you a Bible.

Zhao: I still have that copy of the Bible. I am an atheist, but I have read the Bible. I find the English in the Bible very beautiful. I read it as an English textbook.

Palau: If you are studying it as an English textbook, then you need to make sure you are using a good edition.

Zhao: I'll have my colleague go to my office and bring the Bible here for you to check (*someone brings the* Bible). Here it is.

Palau: That's a good edition, you may use it as an English textbook.

An edition of the Bible approved by Palau

Zhao: Then I'll ask you to sign it for me, just to show that you approve of its English.

PART ONE

On the Bible and God

Cathedral of St. Patrick in New York

Religious books displayed
at Zhongguancun Book
Center in Beijing

Palau: What got you interested in the Bible, since you have a secularist, atheistic background? What made you want to read what the Bible said?

Zhao: When I traveled abroad I found that there is a Bible almost in all the hotel rooms. So out of curiosity I read the Bible. I know, in terms of printing, the Bible ranks number one in the world. That explains its importance. In China, 40 million copies of the Chinese edition of the Bible have been printed. Even for a populous country like ours, this figure is still very high. As a matter of fact, there are a lot of religious works translated and published in China, numbering in their hundreds. You will find them in any larger bookstores in China. In the city of Nanjing, there is a special press solely devoted to printing the Bible.

Palau: I did see many religious books in the bookstores I visited, including those by Mr. Crouch. I also went to the Amity Publishing Company in Nanjing and was impressed by the quantity, the quality, and the distribution across China of the Bible. So I'm very grateful.

You have read the Bible. I would like to know what impressed you most.

Zhao: I started my career as a researcher in nuclear physics. In physics there are only three Newtonian laws, very clear and simple. Compared with them, the Bible is much more complicated. Perhaps we could reduce the Bible to a few basic points, like the Newtonian laws. I suppose these would be enough. One, God is omnipresent, omnipotent and omniscient. God is perfectly good. Two, because of his original sin, man has difficulty communicating with God. Three, God therefore sends Jesus to communicate with man. Four, man must not try to design his own fate but should follow the guidance of Jesus and the Bible.

Palau: That is quite a perfect summary of the main points of the Bible. Even I as an evangelist have not said it with such perfection and accuracy. Of course, there are many other points of the Christian faith, but you have mentioned the more important components. It seems to me you could make an evangelist and that I should not try to convince you. (*laughter*)

Palau visiting Amity Foundation in Nanjing

Zhao: Simple is beautiful. The Newtonian laws are noted for their preciseness and beauty. So is Einstein's famous formula. Simple in form, but meaningful and rich in deduction.

Even from a non—theological point of view, the Bible is an important book and may be understood from many perspectives.

Palau: So would you give your perspective on the Bible? It will educate me.

Zhao: In the first place, the Bible is a classic for Christians, the basis of their creed. It is also a history book since it records the life, the thoughts and wishes of the various peoples who lived in the Middle East during ancient times. The Bible covers the history of not only the Hebrews but also of other peoples like the Egyptians, Canaanites, Babylonians and others who lived in that region of the world. The Bible is not authored by any individual.

It is the crystallization of the wisdom of many peoples for it was passed down from generation to generation as oral history until some 1,300 years later when it was finalized. The Bible represents a very truthful record of life during ancient times. For example, in the Bible there was no mention of tea as it had not been introduced from the East. Nor did the Bible mention smoking because that bad habit didn't exist then.

Palau: That's true. It didn't mention tea, but I am glad you Chinese brought it to the world.

Zhao: The Bible also records the philosophical thinking of those ancient people who tried to answer some fundamental questions, for example, about the origin of humankind and of the universe. One could see that their philosophy, especially religious philosophy, had reached a certain high level. These people tried to use their wisdom to answer those questions of ultimate concern.

Then the Bible is good literature. Integrating Hebrew, Greek and Roman culture, it abounds in beautiful prose, proverbs and poems. What is more, it has formulated many ethical standards for people, then and now. The Bible is well-worth reading from all these perspectives.

Palau: Well, I think you've got a good grasp of what the Bible teaches in an amazing way. You've accurately expressed

The ancient side of Beijing

the essential meaning of the Bible from the writers' perspective. And there is another dimension that I'm sure you've noticed that comes through when you read it all.

From our point of view, the Bible is part of God's total revelation to man. God reveals himself through creation, the beauty of the world. The whole creation speaks of the glory of God and the power of God. So when one looks at creation, you get a picture that God is almighty, that he loves beauty, that he is creative, that he also enjoys himself because of all the birds and the fish and the amazing things in creation. So everything you said about the Bible is absolutely correct. There's that other spiritual dimension that comes through also.

And secondly, God has revealed himself personally. In the *Book of Colossians*, it says about Jesus Christ, "He is the visible image of the invisible God." When a scientist like you is thinking "I want to look at concrete human things so I can understand them," here comes Jesus who says, "Look at me and you've actually seen the character of God." So it's what we call "progressive revelation." It started with physical creation. It progressed to written revelation, the *Scriptures*. And then we see the coming of Jesus Christ as God's final revelation in a personal way. So it's a progressive way of knowing God.

The beautiful thing, since you're a scientist, is that the Bible never really contradicts the true findings of science. Science and the Bible don't contradict each other in their true findings. And my own conviction, of course the conviction of all Christians, is that the Bible is inspired by God, even though the authors wrote freely, God overruled—if you can use that word—so that the end result was what God wanted us to know about him. And this is profoundly logical. Because if God is a personal God, we believe that he created us humans so that we could relate to him. Since he is invisible, he had to reveal himself and he did it in a progressive way. So for a scientist who becomes a true believer in God through Jesus, it's doubly exciting.

For instance, right now in many of the universities, they're beginning to discuss the issue of intelligent design. And they're also talking about the Big Bang Theory. And in Genesis of the Bible, when it says, "In the beginning, God made the heavens and the earth," it speaks like there was a big explosion.

I'll finish with the final point about the Bible. The climax of the revelation is the crucifixion of Jesus Christ and the resurrection because he was the Son of God. You said it so well when you said that there was need of a bridge between God and humans. And that was Jesus Christ. So in your reading you picked up the right message.

Zhao: You said that when the authors wrote the chapters of the Bible, they got revelation from God. I have a different understanding on this point. Since the Bible was written by a group of authors, I think when they wrote the Bible they had wished that there were a God, because had God existed, they would surely feel more comfortable and encouraged. Such a belief could help them resolve many difficulties in the course of their lives and also meet many of their ultimate concerns. Well, compared to 3,000 or 5,000 years ago, they made really big progress. Before the Bible, there were only primitive religions. For example, one of the primitive religions was witchcraft. Such religions had no "Bible" or other scriptures, only the "performance" of "Shamans" on special occasions.

Palau: I am excited about what you just said. Both things I believe were true according to what the Bible says. The authors of the Bible had God in their heart. And St. Peter says that the

Spirit of God came upon them to help them write what needed to be written. And in the Book of Hebrews in the *New Testament*, it says that God spoke many times and in many ways in the past to the ancients so that when there's a hunger for God, God will reveal himself to a person and he did so throughout history. And he's speaking in China and he's speaking in the States and he's speaking in Argentina.

Do you remember Dr. Billy Graham? He visited China about 15 years ago. And he spoke at some church either in Beijing or in Shanghai. I'm not sure where.

Zhao: Both.

Palau: And he talked about Jesus Christ and the cross and the resurrection. Billy Graham's wife was brought up in China. Her father was a medical doctor here in China. In fact, Mr. Graham is praying for my visit here. He knows all about it.

But when he finished speaking that Sunday morning, an elderly Chinese man from the country came up to him. And he said through the interpreter to Mr. Graham, "What was the name of that man who died on the cross that you told us about?" And Mr. Graham said, "His name was Jesus." And the elderly Chinese man said, "I've always believed in him but I never knew his name." In other words, I think he was saying in his heart God had revealed himself to him but he just didn't know the details.

So from the early days of the creation of man and woman, I think God has been revealing himself in people's hearts. But I think he had the Bible written so that people could know what they believe and what they believe in.

Zhao: You have just told me a very vivid story about the elderly Chinese man. We could find many people like that Chinese farmer in many parts of the world. That's the rationale for the existence of religions.

I read the Bible, but I am not a believer. Why? Because I cannot understand God. From my own experience, I cannot appreciate what the Bible said about God being perfectly good and formless. That is to say, "God's existence is beyond our perception and experience." That I cannot understand. I can only understand what exists, what is concrete and substantive. I don't know if God speaks English, French or Spanish. I have no idea what God looks like. Consequently, I cannot understand such a metaphysical concept.

Palau: Precisely so, we need Jesus to help us communicate with God.

Zhao: Aha, I have to be very careful when talking to you. Otherwise you might be leading me to God through your communication.

PART TWO

On the Creation

The Last Judgement (Sistine Chapel)

Former U.S. President George Bush visiting Luji-
azui in Pudong, Shanghai, on Jan. 18, 1994

Palau: I know you were once responsible for the development of Shanghai's Pudong New Area and for its achievements.

Zhao: Talking about Pudong, I recall a new church we built there. It isn't that grandiose but its design is quite intricate. We built the church in Pudong because we thought there would be more and more people coming from abroad and we should satisfy their needs. At the same time, taking into consideration the needs of local people, we also built one Taoist temple and one mosque.

Palau: I'm going to Shanghai next week, and I will make a point of going to that church while in Pudong.

Zhao: We can't do it together this time. When there is a chance, I shall accompany you when you pay a visit there.

Palau: Recently I came upon a speech on religion by Einstein in which he said, "I want to know God's thoughts; the rest are details." He also once said, "Science without religion is lame;

religion without science is blind."

Zhao: He is not only a great physicist, but also a thinker. As a matter of fact, atheists will have no difficulty appreciating the ethics demonstrated in many of the stories in the Bible. I think the conflicting point is in Genesis.

As a matter of fact, the story about the creation of the universe can be found not only in Genesis of the Bible, but also in many countries and among many peoples. In China we also have our own "Genesis," so to speak. I can tell you a Chinese mythological story about the creation of the universe.

Palau: Tell me, please.

Zhao: According to an ancient Chinese legend, the sky and the earth were inseparable and the whole universe was in a chaotic state back in remote ages. A giant named Pangu separated the sky and earth. It took him 18,000 years to accomplish this, rather than in six days as indicated in the Bible. Pangu spent another 18,000 years to create humans and also many other creatures.

Concerning the creation of humans, there is also another Chinese legend. A goddess named Nuwa created them with mud and dust.

Actually these legends were all attempts by our ancestors to answer those fundamental questions about the origin of the universe and humankind.

Palau: But isn't that interesting! So many kinds of things converge there, don't they? The separation of the waters from the earth, that's in Genesis. And man created from the dust; that's

The Creation of Adam (Sistine Chapel)

in Genesis too. You know this may be why the Chinese culture has an affinity with what the Bible teaches and many Chinese are coming to faith because of that background, don't you think perhaps?

Zhao: Well, in China we have different kinds of people and they have different worldviews. Let's continue to talk about my difficulty in understanding Genesis. God said, "Let there be light and there was light." And God separated light from darkness and then he created the sun. But it's difficult for me to understand this sequence of the creation. I would think if God existed he should first create the sun and then separate light from darkness.

Palau: Now we're talking. The Bible says, "God is light and in him there's no darkness at all." And that has a moral quality because when it says that God is light, it's talking about his purity and holiness, that God is perfect. But the sun was created by God to illuminate certain parts of the universe, not all of the vast universe. So light existed before the sun because God is light.

One more point. I'm not a scientist as you know. You're a scientist. I'm a theologian. But there are scientists who say that indeed if the sun were shut down the universe would still have light. And I'll try and find for you some of the books in English where scientists explain that. I think you'd be very excited by that concept.

Zhao: I cannot understand what is said in Genesis about the origin of light. The issue of the origin of light was a very important one for our ancestors. They were very curious and wanted to have an answer.

During Plato's times, the ancient Greeks thought that light came from human eyes. So according to them, there was light wherever the eyes reached. But Plato pointed out that this assessment was not completely correct since light also came from lamps and other objects which emitted light. But he could not answer the question: what is light. Then in the 18th century Isaac Newton declared that light was a particle stream. So there's shade behind a tree when the particle stream was blocked.

But Christiaan Huygens, a contemporaneous scientist of Newton, said that light was a wave motion like the wave motion sent through wireless and water. Experiments had proved that light had the property of diffraction. Therefore there was a contradiction between the views of Newton and Huygens. Probably because Newton commanded greater authority at the time, more people believed in his theory rather than in Huygens'.

But then Albert Einstein came along and he pointed out that both of their assessments were correct. So according to him, light should be regarded as a quantum and acquire the duality of particle and wave. So you see it is quite a complicated process of recognition for the scientist to answer the question what is the origin of light. I think God will not make it so complicated that light has this duality. Scientists later discovered that the transition of an electron in the atomic shell produces light. But for God, it's very simple. "Let there be light and there was light." God solved the whole issue in one sentence, only he said it 2,000 years before those scientists.

Palau: But do you think God didn't reveal it so that scientists could entertain themselves trying to figure it out and understand it?

Zhao: I think you have reconciled a contradiction between scientists and God.

Palau: Scientists today are searching to understand if there is a creator, how does he relate to all the theories of science? And there are very serious scientists studying it deeply. I want to bring it to the moral and spiritual angle.

The concept of light is very important in Chinese culture, isn't it? And Jesus said, "I am the light of the world. If anyone follows me, they will never walk in darkness but will have the light of life." Then on another occasion, he said, "Men love darkness rather than light because their deeds are evil." So he uses the reality of light and shadows and light and darkness that you were talking about. And he gives it a spiritual application. So the day that you as a scientist become a believer in Jesus, you will be the best explainer of these things to the intellectual community.

Zhao: Having been engaged in scientific research for two decades, I am accustomed to sticking to the materialist viewpoint in my epistemology. But this has not prevented me from respecting people who have religious beliefs. On the contrary, it has stimulated my urge to try and understand the significance of religion and its existence. I'm very keen in understanding your views—the views of a refined theist. They can be a very good reference for me when seeking to understand the differences between theists and atheists.

As pointed out by Max Mueller, "He who knows one knows none." If atheists only know atheism and theists only know theism, that means they only know "one" and therefore none. Do you know Max Mueller?

Palau: Yes. He was a German who wrote on comparative religion.

PART
THREE

On Religion and the Spirit

Palau: An atheist can be a very lonely man because, having no connection with a creator, he is very much on his own. I've talked with many atheists, East and West, and they're very lonely people inside. There is a certain lack of peace of mind and heart until you meet your creator.

Do you remember John Paul Sartre, the French philosopher? He said, "Man is alone, abandoned to his own destiny." And that's really an expression of a person that doesn't know God. You feel alone and you feel abandoned to your own destiny.

But if you know God, then you have a point of reference. Where did I come from? Why am I here? Where am I going?

So there is a sense of history: Where is my origin. There is a sense of purpose: Why am I here? And a sense of destiny: Where am I going? What is the future?

Zhao: You have offered very interesting thoughts. What you said reminds me of a true story in Chinese history. More than 2,000 years ago, there were two great philosophers: one is called

Haoliang River in Autumn, painted by Li Tang of Southern Song Dynasty (Collection of Tianjin Museum)

Zhuangzi and the other Huizi. While they were strolling along a bridge across the Hao River, Zhuangzi said, "You see those fish in the water, how happy they are." And the other philosopher countered, "You're not a fish. How could you know those fish are happy or not?" And Zhuangzi answered, "Since you are not me, how could you know that I have no idea of the happiness of those fish?" In the same way, I say: Since you are not an atheist, how could you know that atheists are lonely?

Palau: Because the atheists speak and write and they express their angst, their inner loneliness.

Zhao: That is to say, those authors or speakers you mentioned may be lonely in their heart, but it doesn't mean all atheists are lonely.

I know that when people feel lonely, they look for help from other people. I suppose when Christians are in difficulties, they often think that God is with them and then they will feel more secure and less lonely.

But for me the difficulty of understanding theism is similar to your difficulty in understanding atheism. I think the differences between theism and atheism may be even greater than between those speaking different languages. Because people use different language systems, they also have different ways of thinking. I hope that our dialogue can serve the purpose of bridging different understandings and different thoughts. Unfortunately, this lack of mutual understanding exists not only in the religious areas but also in the cultural areas. And in the West, religion is closely intertwined with culture.

Palau: In some places, it's true. When I said that an atheist is empty, I didn't mean to say that they're completely empty in every area of their life. Intellectually, atheists are usually far more educated than theists. Often an atheist is contented intellectually in his studies and in his books. I was speaking more of spiritual emptiness and loneliness because a person can be intellectually fulfilled, and you obviously are. As you were telling me that your father said you should read a book at least an hour every day and if you do then you'll become a teacher rather than a learner ten years later. I was referring to that inner spiritual loneliness. That's what I was referring to.

So a person can be happy fishing. A fish can be happy swimming in the waters of the intellect but then finds himself on dry land when it comes to the spirit and the soul. Is that reasonable?

Zhao: Well, you have offered a different interpretation of this fish story. As for me, I cannot answer the question; that is whether the fish feels happy. But I know that the fish belongs to a lower species than man. Fish cannot have as many emotions or sentiments as humankind.

Palau: They definitely can't read books in the water, can they?

Zhao: And I even don't know in what form a fish sleeps in water.

Palau: I don't either.

Zhao: Horizontally or vertically? I don't know.

Palau: It never crossed my mind.

Zhao: When my daughter was still very young, she asked me whether a fish slept or not? And I told her, "I don't know whether it does."

Palau: I can't answer that either.

Zhao: Since we have touched upon the issue of loneliness, perhaps from the perspective of comparing Eastern and Western cultures I may offer some insights.

What you were saying is that when one doesn't have re-ligious beliefs, his soul lacks a prop, hence all atheists have a lonely soul. However, religion is a cultural phenomenon. It is wrong to say that a non-believer in religion is uncultured or lacks culture. Similarly, it is wrong to say that a non-believer in religion has no beliefs whatsoever. Furthermore, not all religious

Confucius (551~479 BC)   Socrates (470~399 BC)

believers are happy and not all atheists are lonely at heart. There have been numerous atheists throughout history and there is no evidence that they were all lonely simply because they did not have "that link with God." For example, Confucius, whom we may consider to be an atheist, has had a profound influence on the mind and spirit of the Chinese people, and perhaps even on people in many other lands. He led a hard life. Yet he was full of passion and happiness when he got into a discussion with his students.

Palau: I'd like to hear that. Once you answer that one, could you explain to me what is Confucius' understanding of heaven?

Zhao: Confucius did not give an exact definition of Tian£™. Nor did he elaborate on his understanding of this concept. Rather

---

£™The Chinese concept of Tian is quite different from the western concept of heaven. Yet for lack of a better English word, "heaven" is often used in translation.

 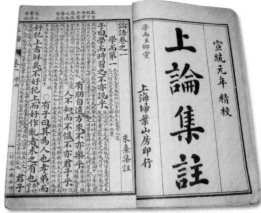

The Analects of Confucius, cover and text

he focused on the relationship between humankind and heaven. Confucius once said, "When I was 15, I began devoting myself to learning. At 30, I could stand on my own. At 40, my mind was no longer confused. At 50, I knew what Tian demanded of me. At 60, my ears were ready for harsh words. Since 70, I have been able to follow my heart's desires without transgressing the rules." Here Tian does not mean Heaven in English. What Confucius meant to say is that one should know his destiny and the rules of Nature and society. Once, his student asked Confucius about the significance of death, and the master answered, "We do not yet understand the significance of life. How can we understand the significance of death?"

Confucius and Socrates lived in more or less the same period in history. The sayings of Confucius and those of other ancient Chinese sages soon spread throughout the country to become part and parcel of traditional Chinese philosophy. Most of the popular ones relate to ethical ideas, though they do not make up their entire ideology. The more profound part of Confucius' philosophy is rather difficult for the average people to comprehend. That also explains why, over these thousands of years, religion has never been dominant in China. To a large extent, it is because of the theories of those ancient Chinese philosophers that the Chinese people have lived in community with each other, and have not broken up into a number of smaller countries as those in Europe and the Middle East.

Palau: That may be a reasonable interpretation. In other words, it leaves a lot of questions, especially the ultimate question, pending and unanswered. Would that be proper to say?

Zhao: The Chinese people answered those ultimate questions in their own ways. It is true that a greater part of the Chinese philosophy focuses on this world, not the other world. Yet, it is also true that they had their own profound thoughts, their own "ultimate concerns." For example, they studied the relations between heaven, earth and man. Buddhists, for example, have always believed in reincarnation. Although many people are not Buddhists, they are deeply influenced by Buddhist ideas and doctrines. Taoism emphasizes harmony between humankind and nature. In modern terminology, this means that man is part of nature. He comes from nature and will eventually return to it.

In ancient times, Chinese emperors attached the greatest importance to their burials. After they died, they were buried in a grandiose and luxurious way, their tombs preserving numer-

Primary school students studying Chinese classics

ous terra cotta pigs, sheep, horses, carts and even with images of their servants. People believed in life in "the neither world." They thought that even after their deaths, they could still ride on their horses and enjoy the meat of their animals in the underworld. That explains, in a way, how the ancients tried to meet their ultimate concerns.

I have found that some religious leaders and those who have had higher learning in theology are very logical in their thinking. This may be a result of the fact that religion lays stress on the study of philosophy.

Palau: Philosophy is the intellectual side of the thinking man. Religion, the spiritual side. It deals with the inner person, the soul, the spirit of the person. We tend to divide in the Bible the human person into three parts: the body, the soul and the spirit. The body is the physical machine. Some atheists feel that that is all there is, just the body, but we believe there is more than the body. There is the soul and spirit.

Much of the human race neglects the spiritual side. Philosophy refers to the soul, the intellect, the thinking and analyzing. But the spirit is that side of the human person that gives you the capacity to actually know God.

St. Paul says that we are spiritually dead until we open our hearts to Jesus Christ. So theology has to do with the spiritual side (Translator's note: The interpreter used the term "ultimate concern" when translating this into Chinese .) while philosophy deals with the soul.

Zhao: You just mentioned the expression "ultimate concern." That expression has been variously translated into Chinese. For your reference, I'll explain from the perspective of an atheist my own view on the soul and spirit.

Atheists do not deny their existence, but our interpretation is different from yours, though there are similarities too. Atheists and theists share the same pursuit in the realm of the soul and the spirit. This strong urge is in no way weakened among the atheists just because they do not have God in their heart. You surely know that at the core of each and every culture there exist a spirit and soul, which is distinguishable from others. Similarly, all societies have their own core values. This fact indicates that the spiritual world and beliefs of both the atheists and theists are rich and firm in conviction. They have differences as well as similarities. That is why they need to communicate with each other, if for no other reason than to "decipher" what each might find difficult to understand of the other.

More than 100 15-year-old high school students from No. 11 Middle School in Zhengzhou City, Henan Province wearing Han Dynasty clothes to observe the so-called "growing up courtesy" in the Confucius Temple on April 5, 2006

Luis Palau with son Andrew and President Bill Clinton (Washington, D.C., 1997)

To a great extent, Chinese philosophy might be described as schools of thought about the relationship between the physical world and the spiritual world. Epistemological materialism does not deny the existence of the spirit, rather it stresses the dialectical relationship between the physical and the spiritual. In China, the building of the material civilization and of the spiritual civilization has always been equally important. We Chinese think that if we have only a physical or bodily existence and have no soul and spirit, then we humans are no different from a cow, sheep or fish.

Philosophically speaking, we need to distinguish between two different concepts: religion and religiosity. A religion has specific teachings, creeds, rituals, believers, churches and clergymen. Religiosity, on the other hand, refers to certain beliefs. For example, someone may believe in Confucianism. He is not a religious believer, but that does not mean he doesn't have any beliefs.

Palau: I was interested in your distinction between religion and religiosity. I often say Christianity is not a religion, because religion is man's efforts to find God and ultimate reality. When we talk about Jesus Christ, we mean that God came down looking for relationship, not a religion.

Zhao: I want to respond to what you have just said. Religion is designed not by God but by human beings who hope in this way to get closer to God in their hearts.

Palau: Yes.

Zhao: As regards the teachings of Confucius and Mencius, some people consider them to be a kind of religion. Actually, Confucianism is not a religion. It is about the basic principles of life and the universe, about moral and spiritual rules. Besides, in Confucianism, there is a lack of theorizing about how the world was created and there are no religious rituals. There are ceremonies commemorating Confucius, but they are not religious in character. The collection of his sayings may be considered to be his doctrines, the most popular of which deal with his ideas about how human beings should live in harmony with each other. Compared with European philosophical writings, his are this worldly. The greater part of European philosophy is devoted to considerations about the laws of things, while Confucius concentrates more on human relationship.

So we can say that Chinese philosophy is closer to the soul and spirit and more flexible. Chinese and European philosophies complement each other.

Performers from various countries participating in the Beijing International Drama Show

Thousand-Hand Avalokitesvara performed by China the Art Troupe of the Handicapped

Cars are entering the homes of millions

The National Theater, one of the ten wonders of new architectures in China selected by the U.S. *Business Week* in 2005

Mencius (372~289 BC)   St. Augustine (354~430)

Palau: Yes, when I began to come to Asia, I studied a bit about Confucianism and Buddhism. I realize what you just said that there is no doctrine of creation in Confucianism and Buddhism. There is no doctrine about God and creation. And the morality of Confucianism and Buddhism in human relations, I think, is excellent, and that's why everybody quotes it. As to what you said about Western Europe, it is only in the last 250 years that Western Europe, in particular, has become materialistic and has no spiritual sense or sense of ultimate eternity at all. Whereas what Jesus brought was revealing the eternal creator to us, so that we can know we are going to live forever. We won't disappear once we die, it is not all over, and we are going to live in eternity.

Zhao: Then people who believe in that will have a more optimistic approach. That will be a great relief to the living, and believers will no longer fear death.

Palau: Yes. And also despair about how short life is because it's all over in 70 years. So people like St. Paul, St. Augustine and myself, we go around and encourage people that there is more to life than just this world. It is not just these 70 or 80 years. There is a glorious future and we are just getting ready for it.

Zhao: About the spirit, I would like to quote Mencius, another ancient philosopher of the Confucian school. He once said, "Life is what I desire, and righteousness is also what I desire. If I cannot have both, I will sacrifice my life for the sake of

A former residence
of Jewish refugees
in Hongkou District,
Shanghai

Museum of Jewish Refugees in Shanghai

President Thomas Krestier, of Austria, accompanied by Zhao Qizheng
during his visit to the former residence of Jews in Hongkou, Shanghai
on Sept. 20, 1995

Zhao Qizheng lecturing in San Francisco, USA, on Sept. 13, 2000

righteousness." (*Mencius*, 2,10) Sometimes you sacrifice your life for the sake of your motherland, sometimes for the sake of other people.

Austrian President Thomas Krestier who died not long ago once told me a tragic story while visiting China. During World War II, at the Auschwitz Concentration Camp, Nazi German officers decided to decimate half of the inmates on the excuse of food shortage. What they did was to do a roll call of the prisoners. Those who had odd numbers would be shot. One of the inmates stood out and said, "I have seven children. I do not want to die." A priest who had an even number said, "I've no children. I'll take your place." Although this priest had never read *Mencius*, what

Dr. Palau preaching to tens of thousands of people at one of his North American Festivals

he did was in complete accord with the sage's teachings. This shows the universality of the noble spirit of humanity.

Palau: Yes, you know from reading the Bible, we all come from one father and one mother, Adam and Eve. So that memory that is imprinted on all of us comes out, in what you said, someone dying for someone else, that is to say, the Christian philosophy of giving your life for somebody else is inside us. We get very emotional when we think that Jesus, the Son of God, would die for us. That makes us weep sometimes, just like the story of the priest. "No one has greater love than this, that someone should give his life for his friends." That is what Jesus said in the Gospel of John. Of course he went a little further and made it hard. He said pray for your enemy and love them. That was pretty hard. But when we were yet the enemies of God, Christ died for us, that is what St. Paul said to the Romans. So God is love.

Zhao: Hence, people of different religions – religious believers and non-believers – should all live together in a peaceful and loving way and not discriminate against each other. That way, we will have a relatively harmonious global village. Our ultimate aim is a harmonious society, a harmonious globe and a harmonious humanity.

Palau: Yes. I have been using that phrase that has now become a Chinese phrase, "a harmonious society."

Zhao: You are well informed about China. The Chinese society traditionally attached great importance to harmony. However, starting from the mid-19th century, China was no longer harmonious because it was too weak and some other countries were too strong, and aggressive wars against China continued endlessly for over a hundred years.

Many of the world's religions are monotheistic, but in China neither Buddhism nor Taoism is so. They are rather tolerant and do not discriminate against other religions. As a matter of fact, in Buddhism, the Buddha is different from the gods. I cannot agree with those extremists who look upon non-believers and believers in other religions as heretics and therefore their enemies.

Palau: It is very dangerous to look upon all atheists and believers of other religions as heretics. It is a horrible thought because it will spread terror among the people. The relationship between God and humans is not like that between humans and computers. Humans must be free to go their own way, otherwise they will become computers. We must not turn humans into robots.

Zhao: Atheists believe that all humans are free. The Bible says God is almighty. If he is almighty why can't he stop all the evils and natural disasters like the tsunamis?

Palau: You have raised a very important point. We should not blame God for giving us the free will when humans are burdened with evil. God is our friend and evil comes from the heart of humans. As to the tsunamis, we can exchange views and take time to think about it further, but we may never know why God allows tsunamis until we get to heaven. Perhaps, God uses disasters to wake up the world and draw attention to our indifference.

Zhao: But the price is too high. I've discovered a collection of Augustine's works. He used theodicy to explain the coexistence of God and evil, but his arguments aren't as convincing as yours. Maybe you can write your own theodicy. I've here the Chinese translation of his works, with a drawing of him. I shall let you have it if you like.

Palau: Then, please sign your name for me too. Thank you very much.

This is my latest one, entitled *High Definition Life*. It is a book about a better life. Instead of settling for the good, we need to do the best, the clearest life possible.

Zhao: Oh, *High Definition Life*, the best life possible. The more common term used in physics for "definition" is "resolution". But sometimes digital life might be too tiring for human beings.

Palau: Yes, that's true. They can sleep on it. You need a system to help you.

Zhao: While digital life brings many conveniences, too many figures and codes make it hard for your mind to register.

On Religious Beliefs in China

A temple fair in Beijing

Palau: Overseas, there are many different ideas on how many Christians live in China. In the United States, we hear that there are 120 to 160 million very serious Christians in China. Is that figure accurate? What percentage of the Chinese population is influenced by Buddhism?

Zhao: There are about 16 million Christians in China. Some others may have such beliefs. However, since they do not take part in religious activities, there is no way to include them in the statistics. There are also many Buddhists in China, but because they do not practice baptism or other rituals, it's difficult to cite their exact number in China. I should add that many people here are influenced by Buddhism to varying extents. During the Spring Festival, for example, normally 50,000 to 100,000 people go to a very famous Buddhist temple in Shanghai on the very first day of the festival. These people may believe in the Buddha,

A foreign visitor fascinated by the Chinese pinwheel

A devout Buddhist believer

though they don't call themselves Buddhists. Broadly speaking, the number of religious believers totals over 100 million in China. You will find these figures in the books I gave you. Also, religious believers and non-believers have been at peace with each other for centuries.

Palau: To remember the ancestors, is that why some people go to the temple?

Zhao: People go to the temples with different wishes. But most pray for the happiness of their families, for their own good health and prosperity, and also to show respect for the ancestors.

Palau: I have traveled in a hundred countries. I would like the world to know that there are so many in China who actually are believers in Jesus as well as other religions. I think it would be good to the communication of what China really is and for the world to know that. Would you authorize me to do that?

Zhao: Sure, we will be very happy if you do so.

Palau: I think the world needs to understand that in China, people are free to believe, and millions upon millions do believe, for instance, in Jesus and in Christianity. I think it is good for the world to know that this is a reality. Just now, you mentioned that there are millions of Christians and hundreds of millions of religious believers in China. Many Americans don't realize that, for instance, the Bible is published in China—40 million copies have been published already. It's available in the bookstores and at a very low price.

What I'm noticing is the tremendous change in the spiritual atmosphere of China. Over one hundred thousand churches, temples, monasteries and mosques that are all over the country. I've learned that there are two new churches that have just been built in Beijing. I have been impressed by the quality of the Christianity that is proclaimed by all the churches in China.

I've met also with some unregistered church leaders and therefore I was impressed by their enthusiasm for all the good things happening in China.

Zhao: There is a Chinese saying that "it is better to see something once than hear about it a hundred times."

We can now touch upon a topic which is somewhat related to politics. Now in Europe and especially in the United States, there are many misunderstandings about China's reality, about its political situation, its religion and press systems. To put all these misunderstandings and attacks into one basket, they are directed against our human rights situation. However, I think no country in the world can claim to have a perfect record in this respect, and the United States and China are no exception. If we humans have a perfect record, then there is nothing left for God to do, and we no longer have to make any efforts.

Palau: That's a good point. No one country can claim to be perfect, but we all must be working toward perfection. One thing I want to say is that we don't confuse the press with the public. In the United States, the general public has a very critical view of the news media. They have more than freedom of the press, they have chaos of the press.

Zhao: Well, sometimes creating news about chaos is in the interest of the press, because they can make more money out of it.

Palau: But they can create a lot of trouble for the government.

Zhao: Governments and religious leaders should not allow themselves to be manipulated by the press, since the newspapers and magazines are often designed by chief editors closeted in their offices. These people design their political "events" in the same manner as fashionable colors are designed by the clothing business. Unfortunately, some politicians frequently succumb to the pressure of the press and/or even manipulate the press. In both cases, they go against the will of God.

Palau: Yes, I absolutely agree with that. God believes in truth, not in lies. I would like, in any way I could, to communicate the truth, facts on the spiritual and Christian side of China. You know, telling people the truth instead of allowing the lies to go on.

Zhao: This is an excellent idea.

Palau: Is there any way that I could be of help, in the United States, in the West, or in Latin America?

Zhao: There are many things you can do. Language-wise, Chinese is spoken by more people than any other language. However, there are only a few countries using Chinese. Therefore, from the language perspective, it is quite difficult to spread Chinese-language publications and movies in Latin America and the United States. This is not only due to language barriers but also because there are cultural differences. We have to rewrite our publications in a way that is acceptable to the Americans and Latin Americans. This is a rather difficult task for us.

I think you can serve as a bridge by helping us to communicate with people of other cultures. Once we establish cultural communication, political and economic communication becomes possible. While China abounds in cultural and natural sights, we cannot expect all Americans and Latin Americans to come to China as tourists. We have already produced many DVDs about these sights. If you could turn these DVDs into your own

Christian believers of Miao nationality

A girl with a Miao language edition of the Bible

language and make them available locally, that would be a great help to us. Alternatively, you could send photographers here to produce your own DVDs covering life in China or scenic and cultural sights.

Five thousand years ago, the earliest forms of the Chinese language appeared and about three thousand years ago, it was already fully developed. The different dynasties already had their official historians. So China has been able to keep rather detailed records of its past. The artifacts unearthed can often match with those historical records. However, due to damages caused by wars and natural disasters, there are also some artifacts that cannot be explained fully. For example, the Sanxingdui Culture discovered in Sichuan Province was very much like the Maya Civilization, yet because of a lack of written record, we have yet to establish a solidly based explanation for its existence and significance.

Mysteries like this are the common heritage of mankind. We have already produced films and DVDs of these sights, but we have not been able to distribute them in the United States or in Latin America. If you are interested in them, I can present you with a set. Although they are in Chinese, you will get a feel of the beautiful scenery and you would probably be able to see more viewing the DVDs than you could as a tourist.

Palau: Yes, absolutely. Recently I read that tombs of Christians have been discovered in China, dating from the year 92 of the Gregorian Calendar. I thought it very interesting when I read about this.*

In the US, Europe and Latin America, there is such an interest in China that I am sure these DVDs when translated into English would be very helpful. I am going too see Dr. Pat Robertson next week and then Mr. Paul Crouch sometime in July. I'll talk to them about this to see what can be done because they've got all the first-class television equipment.

Zhao: That's fine. I am presenting you with a set of DVDS produced by the Intercontinental Media Center. They give you an idea of Chinese historical heritages like the Hemudu Culture,

---

* According to one historian, in A.D. 635 the Persian Bishop Alopen, a Nestorian Christian, made official contact with the Chinese at the capital city of Chang-an, and in the 13th century, Genghis Khan asked the Pope to send 100 Christian scholars to China to teach the people about Christianity—but almost ten years later, a new Pope sent only two representatives.

Copper statue of ancient Shu people excavated from the Sanxingdui site in Sichuan Province

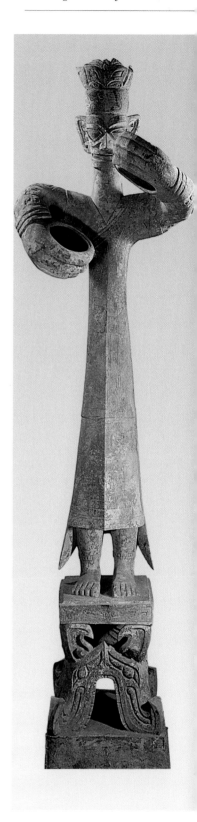

Sanxingdui Culture and the Terra Cotta Warriors of the First Emperor of Qin. If you don't mind lugging them along, here are two volumes of *Religions in China*. They are rather heavy but I suppose it is God's will, not to make you suffer but to make you happy.

Palau: Sure, I'll definitely be reading them. Thank you.

I have a suggestion. Why don't we take the recording and put out a book on our discussion today?

Zhao: No problem at all. We shall put in a few footnotes. You will indicate where the quotes from the Bible come from and I'll do the same for *The Analects* by Confucius and *Mencius*.

Palau: That's wonderful. We could call it a face-to-face communication between an American and a Chinese. A communication that is quite profound.

Zhao: We could call it "a dialogue between an atheist and a theist." *

Palau: I like this title. We had a very good conversation today.

---

* At Dr. Palau's suggestion, the book was later named *Riverside Talk—A Dialogue between an Atheist and a Christian*.

Terra-Cotta warriors excavated in Xi'an, Shaanxi Province

I want to tell you when I dreamed of coming to China as a little boy, my mother read me stories about China. And we used to pray for China. I always said I wanted to come to China through Shanghai, because one of the stories was by a doctor from England called Dr. Hudson Taylor. He loved China. He built hospitals and schools in China during the 1800s. I think he came in through Shanghai. Once, when I was in Hong Kong, they offered to bring us to the mainland through Guangzhou. But I said no, I'm coming to China through Shanghai. In 2000, finally I came into China through Shanghai. My dream came true.

Zhao: You are right. Shanghai is the key to modern China.*

Palau: I am afraid you are a little prejudiced about Shanghai. Thank you for your generous time for I know how busy you are. Will we stay in touch?

Zhao: That's for sure. Let's fix another time and place for the next meeting.

---

* Minister Zhao spoke English here. He was quoting the title of a book with this title written by Prof. Ross Murphy of the University of Maryland published in 1953.

PART FIVE

On Chinese and Western
Cultures and Philosophy

Shanghai at night

November 16, 2005,
Regal International East Asia Hotel, Shanghai

Zhao and Palau signing the Memo of Understanding on the Shanghai Talks on Nov. 17, 2005

Palau: Well, it's good to be in your city. I'm excited to meet with you today and the last conversation was so thrilling too. I've always had a high regard for a person who says he is an atheist because at least it shows he is thinking about spiritual issues and whether there is a God or there isn't a God. Too many religious people are religious because their fathers and grandfathers were religious. They just go along with the current. But atheists are thinking and they are challenging the status quo and therefore it's fun to discuss with an atheist. An atheist and a Christian have one thing in common: we think hard. So I am anxious to get going today.

Zhao: I'm very happy too. To know a Christian leader who has such profound ideas like you is a personal honor.

Right now in the world there are about two billion Christians and more than one billion non-religious believers. Starting from the 1960s, many have advocated dialogues between different religious groups. This is very important. But we should not neglect dialogues between religious and non-religious people. Enhanced mutual understanding between theists and atheists is conducive to the harmony of the world.

Palau: Absolutely, I agree with that. When you talked to me last May, you brought up a very interesting subject that we weren't able to develop. And I wondered about your thoughts on this because I know that many people in China have this thought, and I always wanted to hear the views from someone who thinks, like you do.

I think you asked, "Why are there demons or evil spirits in the world if God is good?" I would love to hear your response to that. And the masses are afraid of being cursed by evil spirits, aren't they? What's the meaning of that?

Zhao: Just like people in other countries, the Chinese people have their fears and worries. They are afraid of natural disasters like earthquakes, tsunamis and influenza. They are also afraid of accidents, such as traffic and other accidents. Additionally, there are so-called man-made disasters – for example, robbery and murders. Even worse than these is war.

During the 9.11 event some 3,000 people in the United States lost their lives. China lost 35 million people during the 14-year

War of Resistance Against Japanese Aggression (1931-1945). Many families suffered deaths during that war. Some families were wiped out. As a result, we still have very vivid memories of those terrible wars. So we can say that every Chinese person is very vigilant about the peril of war in the world today.

When we look back on our contemporary history, we can see that the Chinese people have been victims of war. We have never launched wars against other countries but we have been invaded on many occasions. We think that those who launched wars are demons, criminals of the worst sort. In China we have a saying, "Be clear on whom to love and whom to hate." That means we should love the people and hate the demons, particularly those who launch wars.

So it is rather difficult for the Chinese people to understand why we should love our enemies, as indicated in the quote from the Bible, "love your enemy". If the enemies have been taken prisoners we will treat them in a humanitarian way, but we cannot say we should love our enemies. And we cannot understand why when your enemy already slaps you on the right cheek, you should turn your left cheek to him. It is extremely difficult to imagine that New Yorkers, for example, should love those terrorists who launched attacks on 9.11.

Palau: Do you want me to answer that one? Here's a thought. I think when Jesus says that we are to love our enemies he's speaking about our personal attitude towards the enemy.

Zhao Qizheng at the opening ceremony of "A Trip of Chinese Culture to the United States" on Sept. 5, 2000

And what you were saying about hating your enemy in the sense when they attack you, that is an official response to evil. So personally, because I've done evil things, though I didn't start any wars, I can therefore sympathize with evil people, forgive them, and pray for them personally.

But if I'm the police chief of Shanghai or the top general in the Chinese Army or the president or Prime Minister of China, then I have an official responsibility to defend the country, whatever it takes. So we can simultaneously hold both things and both are true.

If I'm spiritually developed, I can say, "God, have mercy on this evil person," and I forgive them. But since I've got power to defend my country, I've got to go after them—so the ying and the *yang*. On the one hand, I can say, "Okay, I'm going to pray for this evil person. God have mercy on him." But as a person in authority – boom. That's how I see that expression "love your enemy" in the Gospel of Jesus.

Zhao: So that means God may forgive the evil persons, but I will not necessarily do so on justified grounds. Is that so?

Palau: It takes a lot of spiritual growth to forgive someone who's done a really evil thing against you.

Zhao: Following your logic, can I say that if someone is a committed Christian and a police chief at the same time, then he may be in a dilemma because of his "double capacity"?

Palau: That's true. I have an experience that happened in London, England. We had a football stadium full of people. And right in the middle of the program, a group of animal rights people interrupted the whole thing running right through the stadium. Some of them were naked. And the stadium was full of men, women, and boys and girls. The policeman that was standing behind me was the police officer who was protecting me. He immediately recognized who was the leader of this group interrupting the whole stadium meeting. And he cried out loud. "That's Billy. I'm going to get him." So he walked off the platform, ran after this fellow Billy, tackled him hard, and got him out of the stadium. Other policemen came and took all the other bunch. So he took care of the problem hard.

But then he felt guilty that night. So he called up this fellow Billy and he said, "Billy, come back tomorrow night to the stadium. I will sit with you. I will take you to dinner. But I want you to hear the message." So, in a way, he did both things, didn't he?

Zhao Qizheng accompanying Warren Christopher, Secretary of State of the United States, and James Sasser, U.S. ambassador to China, on the west bank of the Huangpu River in Shanghai the development of Puding, Watching, on Nov, 21, 1996

Zhao: You have just told me a vivid story you personally experienced. Sometimes people have to choose between loving the majority of people or a number of people and loving a single person. Those with a sense of justice should choose to love the majority of people. In China, we have a strict definition of who the enemy is. Here the enemy refers to those who are hostile to one's country and people. For example, we refer to those Japanese troops during World War II as enemies, but we do not count people like Billy in your story as enemies. For example, even up until today, the Jewish people cannot forgive those Nazi officers in the Auschwitz Concentration Camp. They are still trying to chase those Nazi officers. And for the Chinese people, they cannot forgive those Japanese war criminals since the latter killed millions of Chinese people. But the Chinese people have already forgiven those ordinary Japanese soldiers although they also killed the Chinese people.

Palau: I think in a way it's judicial action and personal attitudes. Judicially, we hate evil and those who have done it have to pay for their evil. That's the judicial side. And then personally you can do what you just said. You can say, "I forgive you. You were following orders but it was evil what you did."

Forgiveness has to be the highest level of spiritual development, I think. Because as you read in the Bible, it says, "God so loved the world that he gave his one and only Son; that whoever believes in him should not perish or be punished but have eternal life." So God had that dilemma with us human beings.

God as judge had to deal with us harshly because we've broken his laws. But because God also is love and he's a loving Father he found a way to forgive us judicially. And that's the mystery of the crucifixion of Jesus Christ. Because it was God taking upon himself the punishment that the human race deserved so as to be able to forgive us and make us new people. It's a profound thought. But that's what the cross is about.

Zhao: In China, we also give humanitarian treatment to criminals. Of course we treat those criminals first according to law, but we also show love and concern for them. While in prison, they can still learn new knowledge and skills. In other words, we believe in the power of education. Those who mistreat prisoners are educated and/or punished, depending on the seriousness of the mistreatment.

It is a great spirit to sacrifice one's life for the interest of the people. We can find numerous such cases in both China and the United States: those people sacrificed their lives for the interest of their own country or for the common interest of humankind. Some died in battlefields, others died in the prisons of their enemies.

Veterans of the Flying Tiger on a visit back to Yunnan

During World War II, although the war was not fought on U.S. territory, hundreds of American volunteers came to China to fight the aggressors. They were very courageous and many died in battle. We shall always remember those who sacrificed their lives for the cause of human justice.

Palau: Do you remember in the Gospel of John Jesus said, "No one has greater love than this that someone should give his life for his friends." It's very touching, isn't it, when somebody gives his life for somebody else.

The other day in the United States they appointed General Peter Pace as Chairman of the Joint Chiefs of Staff. When he accepted the position on television nationally, he told this little story. He said, "I wouldn't be here today if it wasn't for a fellow marine during the Vietnam War." He said, "I was a lieutenant and I had about 20 men who fought with me. I remember one day when we were in a foxhole. And one of my men walked in front of me. At that moment a bullet hit him and he died right in front of me." And he added, "That bullet was coming straight here," Pointing to his chest.

Even though he's such a tough military man, he had tears in his eyes. He said, "He died for me. He died in my place." And in a sense that's what God did on the cross. He took the bullet that we deserved for breaking the law and gave us forgiveness and eternal life.

Zhao: In China's ethical tradition, we put a special emphasis on *Yi*, which means justice or integrity in English. We Chinese emphasize that for the cause of justice one should be ready to "surmount mountains of knives and swim in the sea of fire". We have our own understanding of the significance of death. "To die for the people is weightier than Mount Thai," a famous mountain in China. The man who made this remark was Chairman Mao Zedong. It has been spread extensively in China, becoming a very popular adage. We Chinese therefore have a special respect for those who sacrifice their lives for the interest of the majority of people.

Palau: That's the beautiful side—the positive side—of human nature, isn't it?

Zhao: We hold that human beings must have a sense of ethics. Mencius once said, "Revere the elders in other families as you do your own elders; love the children in other families as you do your own children." (*Mencius*, 1.7)

Luis Palau with President George W. Bush, First Lady Laura Bush, Reverend Yu Xinli and Liu Hongliang in front of the Gangwasi Church in Beijing in November 2005

Palau: Jesus said something similar to what you have just quoted, "Love your neighbor as yourself." Our education is pretty similar in this respect.

You have said that there are many similarities between the ethical ideas of Confucius and Mencius and those of the Christian religion. One of the reasons why there are so many common truths may be because we all came from the same source. Chinese thought is especially meaningful because your civilization is over 5,000 years old.

Zhao: I find that actually we have much common ground. At the same time we also have different ideas. Just because of these differences, our dialogue becomes more significant. If I had a dialogue with my shadow, I would be exhausted in the end. I would lose interest in such a dialogue.

Palau: I would too.

Zhao: We grew up with totally different backgrounds. That makes our dialogue fresh and interesting. We can always find some fresh ideas and talking points in our conversation. In the process of our dialogue, we can enhance our mutual understanding. Dialogue is the best means to overcome cultural obstacles.

With the invention of jumbo-jets and satellite television and the popularization of the Internet, the world has become much smaller. Contacts and exchanges between East and West have grown tremendously. Only 200 years ago, many Chinese had no idea that the United States existed.

Palau: I read it in your book, the speech you gave at the National Press Club in the United States, when you said that very point. *

Zhao: That book expressed the Chinese people's friendship with the American people. Exchanges between the East and West become ever closer. Mutual understanding between them becomes more and more necessary. It is important for us to understand what we have in common and where we are different from each other. We have to understand that it is entirely reasonable that we have those differences. Mutual understanding is not an easy thing, of course. Many people do not have the opportunity as we have today to have a straightforward and unrestrained exchange of ideas.

America and Americans through Chinese Eyes, by Zhao Qizheng, China Intercontinental Press, Chinese and English editions.

If the Chinese people understand the United States only from those mega movies, then they will think that there is much violence in the United States – so many heroes and gangsters and bandits. If the American people understand China also from those movies, they will think that in China people still keep the long pigtail and most of them practice martial arts. That is very far from the truth.

Palau: The film industry has probably done more harm for the image of the United States in the world than anything else.

I used to live in South America, in another country, not my own country, and they're real macho, real manly guys. There was a movie that came from Hollywood to this South American country about doctors' wives. According to this movie, doctors' wives in the United States were very lonely women; that the medical doctors are so busy they ignore their wives. And according to this movie they're desperate for a man. So all over this country they used to say, "Take me to the U.S.A. I'll take care of those doctors' wives." But it's the image that they project all over the world, not only violence but ridiculous sex. The impression is that America is nothing but a big brothel.

Zhao: I would think the film director and the scriptwriter are not Christians.

Palau: Oh, that's for sure. You can sign on that one. Yeah.

Zhao: That means those people sacrificed justice for the sake of personal interest.

Palau: Yeah. But mostly it's money. Whatever makes money, people think it's alright. But some people don't know the distinctions nowadays between reality and filmmaking. It's one of the dangers that you see a movie and you see a dialogue

Dr. Palau preaching

and it's so real that you think you were talking to your friend last week.

One day one of my boys when he was little said to me, "Dad, is this real or is it just a movie?" And that's being blurred today: reality and illusion.

Zhao: But for those absurd movies, they may make big profits out of them, and serious movies only have a small audience. Perhaps you can give me a list of serious movies in the future. I won't bother with those not on your list.

Palau: The list won't be very long.

Zhao: Precisely, because there are differences between the culture of the East and that of the West. We need to strengthen our cultural interflow. When we talk about the West, we refer mainly to Europe and the United States. Since the ancestors of the American people came from Europe, you are very close. But then, for the East, it's a different story. It is so big. We have many different countries with different religions and different civilizations.

In Asia, we can at least list the following major civilizations: China, India, the Middle East and Japan. In the Middle East, the culture is diversified and there are many conflicts there. In Asia, China and India have maintained quite healthy economic development and Japan, of course, is already a developed country. Therefore the Western countries are paying more attention to Asia, including its cultures.

Exchanging gifts

The Western countries are already quite developed economically and they are exporting high technology and capital to other countries. So the Eastern countries study and learn from the West more than the West studies the East. In other words, the East knows more about the West than vice-versa.

Over the past two decades, China has increased its contacts and exchanges with Western countries. During the initial stage, even in business negotiations, it was quite difficult and time-consuming to reach common understanding since both sides were unfamiliar with the other side's customs and way of thinking. But now, the situation has much improved since now we know much more about each other's cultural background. We are much more efficient in our negotiations with less cost and better results. And that's not only true in the business area; we have similar cases in the political area.

PART SIX

On Religion and Science

Hongen Hall, a new Catholic church in Pudong, Shanghai

Palau: And the spiritual, because the spiritual and religious underlines our attitudes to life, doesn't it? What we believe is important because it touches on every area of life.

The very week following 9.11, we were having a festival on the beach in a town south of San Francisco in California. Everybody was still in a state of shock over the twin towers in New York. And that night on the beach, there was a family, a father, mother and two teenage girls. They were in charge of making sure that the beach was clean after the evening festival. They were going back in their car at 11:00 at night when a big SUV van hit theirs and the two teenage girls died on the spot. I went to the hospital to see the father and mother. And to the crowd who was aware of the accident, I reminded them that when it is a dramatic thing like the Twin Towers, or the tsunami in Indonesia, we're all alarmed. But in fact, every day, quietly, people are dying from old age, or diseases, or accidents. Every day – 160,000.

So one of my roles is to remind people we must get ready for eternity because life on earth is only 70, 80 or 100 years, and then eternity. At that point, all science and knowledge and poetry and politics are behind us. So I see my role as somebody blowing the trumpet, waking people up about eternity. That's my privilege.

Zhao: I think it's a beautiful idea to care about life and to seek eternity. If there is truly eternal life, I think everybody would welcome it.

But then, I think a new problem emerges. Since there are more and more people born on this earth and if more and more acquire eternal life, how could so many of them be accommodated in heaven? Buddhism offers a solution, for according to Buddhism, there is reincarnation, so reincarnation can solve this problem. But the question is: why are there still more and more people on the earth even though there is reincarnation?

Palau: I don't even want to try and guess that one.

Zhao: I've raised this question with some Buddhist high priests. They can't seem to give me a clear answer, either. Maybe it's just me who can't understand. I began to think with the passage of time, will there be a need for the Bible and the Buddhist scriptures to be amended? Not in terms of the language but in terms of supplementing the content. Otherwise, they cannot answer the questions posed by science with the emergence of new concepts, new theories and new facts. Theologians need to offer interpretations for those new ideas and theories; in other words, to meet the challenges presented by the development of science. So I'm wondering whether the theologians will get a

A street scene in Beijing

The CBD in Beijing

Palau trying out on the Chinese instrument *pipa*

new revelation from God and amend the Bible and there will be a new edition of the Bible?

Palau: I don't think so, but let me tell you a story. The Director of NASA in Houston, Texas—NASA is the one that sends the satellites to the moon and into planetary space—this fellow happened to be a Christian, one of the directors of NASA, and a very serious scientist. He said, "I think history is like three mountains, each one higher than the previous one. And the scientists are crawling up the first mountain and they don't find the answer. They climb the second mountain, they reach the top and they still can't find the answer. And then the scientists climb the third mountain and they're tremendously surprised. There sit all the theologians laughing at them."

Zhao: I think there are not only three mountains. There are countless mountains. With each mountaintop you scale, you

The famous Bund by the
Huangpu River in Shanghai

Zhao and Palau cruising on the
Huangpu River on Nov. 17, 2005

will find some relative truth. The higher the mountain, the closer you are to absolute truth. But no one person can scale so many mountains during a lifetime. Maybe only one or two. So it is the mission of generation after generation to continue climbing the mountains, never ending.

Palau: That's right. And when it comes to science and technology and human knowledge, it keeps expanding. We keep searching and studying and seeking to know and that's right. But eventually when we get to the ultimate truth, we say, "Ah! It was God."

Zhao: From the theologian's perspective, it is quite simple to answer the question of ultimate truth. A very simple answer: It is God.

Palau: Yes.

Zhao: The core of theology is the existence of God, and the

Hongen church

basis of theology is the Bible. I doubt if humankind can find the ultimate truth. We can only work to approach it steadily.

Scientists and theologians have different definitions of truth. This is quite a complicated issue. Even among atheists as well as among theists, many have different definitions of truth, just as there are different definitions of religion among theologians.

Palau: Yes. There is material truth, mathematical truth, and philosophical truth. But above it all is God. Now it doesn't stifle scientific inquiry. Believing in God actually helps a scientist enjoy his research even more. To put it simply: The Bible doesn't say to the scientist, "Believe in God, shut your mouth and shut off your brain." The Bible says to the scientist, "Believe in God, the Creator, and enjoy the search for different truths of creation."

Zhao: Well, in our view, besides such sciences as mathematics, physics and chemistry, it is also the mission of philosophy to explore the ultimate truth. Hegel, the famous German philosopher, once said, "Philosophy is like Minerva's owl which sets out only at sunset." I think what he means, firstly, is that philosophy is a reflection on things which have already happened concerning the universe, the earth, humankind, and individuals, and on that basis, extract the truth. Secondly, he was saying that the owl can fly high and see far. It can even see in the dark.

Philosophers should also have such abilities. I think the significance of philosophy lies in reflecting over the past, and from that, drawing conclusions to guide actions in the future.

In the beginning of the last century, the Chinese translation of the word "philosophy: was zhi xue, literally meaning "science of wisdom". That means people should transcend existing knowledge to reach a higher level of thinking and logic.

Palau: It is interesting. The word "philosophy" itself is from two Greek words: philo is love and sophia in Greek is wisdom. So the original meaning of the Greek word philosophia, or philosophy, is a combination of love and wisdom.

Zhao: I understand "love of wisdom" also to mean "love of truth".

Palau: Yes, seek truth and enjoy life.

Zhao: Truth is also a kind of beauty. People can enjoy the beauty of searching for and finding the truth. There are many kinds of beauty—the beauty of nature, beauty of paintings, of music, of architecture and so on. A philosopher will find beauty in philosophy, when after reflecting, he gains new ideas. Such beauty is of a very sophisticated kind. For instance, there is the famous equation $E=mc^2$ formulated by Albert Einstein. Einstein saw it as a beautiful equation, because it not only, in very simple terms, showed the relationship between matter and energy, but also embodied philosophical meaning.

Palau: I read that and I have no idea what he's talking about. It's beyond me.

Zhao: Well, to put it simply, before Einstein, physicists thought energy and matter were two separate things. But Einstein's equation proved that the two are transferable.

Palau: Why doesn't matter explode? What keeps it from exploding when there's energy going all the time?

Zhao: Certain matter needs certain qualities and external conditions before it can transform into energy and explode.

Palau: So that's when the oxygen and atoms in an atomic bomb collide and it explodes.

Zhao: There are two kinds of nuclear reactions. One is called fusion and the other fission. I suddenly find that you have quite a high faculty for understanding physics.

Palau: So when you scientists get to the top of the mountain, we theologians will be sitting there laughing. And we will have equal understanding.

Zhao: But scientists have already sent some equipment to Mars and that's much higher than the mountains.

Palau: No. No. We're in heaven. We're above Mars.

Zhao: In fact, the scientists and the theologians have their own mountains. They should co-exist in friendship and greet each other from their mountains. The distance between them should get narrower and narrower rather than wider and wider.

The spacecraft Shenzhou-6 launched successfully on Oct. 12, 2005

Beijing Spectrometer is a huge facility to detect different particles produced in BEPC

Three-Gorges Dam opening its gates to discharge flood waters for the first time after its construction on July 18, 2006

The newly-constructed Qinghai-Tibet Railway known as the "Heavenly Road"

Performance of China Buddhist Music and martial art in San Francisco, USA

Miss World Competition held in Sanya, Hainan Province

Weifang International Kite Festival in Shandong

And that needs dialogue.

Palau: Yes, you're right.

Zhao: We've both tried to make clear our own viewpoints. Our dialogue has enhanced our mutual understanding. That's our common achievement.

Palau: You've made me think of something I've never thought about before. You're an architect, a scientist, a philosopher, and soon you're going to be a theologian. Yeah, you. But I'm thinking, theologians come from the top down. The scientists are from the bottom up and we're getting close to meeting in the middle.

Zhao: There are philosophers who don't believe in God. Their field is to study the philosophy of religion. Are there theologians who do not believe in God, who study theology or a certain religious philosophy?

Palau: Okay, you like definitions. "Theologian" means theo logos, knowledge of God. It's another Greek double word. Theo is God, logos is knowledge. So a theologian is one who knows God. A theologian who doesn't believe in God is not a theologian in the sense of the word. How can you know God and not believe in him?

Zhao: What I mean is we can regard religion and study theology from the philosophical perspective. In fact, atheists have been using many religious terms but often with not completely the same implications. There are huge differences between the Chinese language and Greek and English. It is easier to translate from Greek into English and still keep the phonetic traces of the original. Not so if you are translating it into Chinese. There would be no traces of the original phonetics left. That's a unique feature of the Chinese language. Even for our dialogue today, we have a language problem. Translating Chinese philosophical ideas into English is very difficult. Different translators translating the same book may come up with two quite different English versions as though they were two different books.

Palau: But China has enormously brilliant theologians. I know some of them, who really understand the Eastern mind, the Middle Eastern mind, and the West. And the brilliant thing about the Bible is that it fits every culture. The Bible fits the Western mechanical, mathematical machine but it also fits the Eastern philosophical, more religious mindset

And these Chinese theologians that I've met, I've met them through the years studying in the West but also in Singapore and Hong Kong, and here in the mainland of China. I haven't yet mingled enough but they're very, very bright. Very gifted. I believe this next century is China's century, not only in terms of good Chinese enterprise, science, and technology, but also in the study of theology and the Bible.

Zhao: For China, Christianity is an imported item. It's not a local product. Buddhism is also imported from abroad, but it has long been localized so as to make it more compatible with Chinese culture.

Palau: I've got to say something. Actually, Christianity was imported from heaven to every nation. When Jesus was born of the Virgin Mary, Christ brought in Christianity and it's an important religion for every culture, not just China.

Zhao: Most of the major religions claim that theirs is the only God. I cannot discriminate against anyone of them. So I am left with only two choices. The first: I believe all their claims are correct. In that case, there will be many gods. The second choice is: all the claims are unfounded; there's no God at all. No religion would agree with me on that, either.

Palau: It's too easy to answer that one. There's no God? Forget it. You got to get serious and say, "I'm going to find God if it's the last thing I do." You're a scientist, you have to dig, dig, dig.

Zhao: Digging, or thinking, requires only a good brain, but it's very difficult to set up a special laboratory to test whether there is a God and which god is the true God. We have not yet found the facilities and methods required for such a laboratory.

Palau: Now you've said the right thing. You are the laboratory. Jesus says, "Minister Zhao, if you will open your heart to me, I will come into your life, forgive all your mistakes and

Deng Xiaoping inspecting BEPC (Beijing Electron Positron Collider)(1988)

BEPC is a large facility for the research of High Energy Physics and the application of Synchrotron Radiation .Many achievements have been obtained by BEPC since 1988. Photo shows BEPC tunnel

all your sins, give you peace in your conscience. I will send my Spirit into your life. I will give you the assurance of eternal life. I will answer your prayers. I will guide your path. I will bless you in every way. I will set you free from the vices that you may have secretly." So there's the laboratory, Dr. Zhao.

Zhao: If I have a laboratory for testing the existence of God, I will, in my laboratory, say to Jesus "If you really exist, please reveal yourself. Give me a signal to indicate your existence." But he will not answer me.

Physicists find their answers in laboratories and theologians find their answers in churches. There are big differences between laboratories and churches. If I install my equipment in a church, I wonder if the results would be different.

Palau: It's getting more and more interesting. I think tomorrow morning, we can continue our dialogue about the relationship between science and religion, starting with the church and the laboratory. I think our dialogue is extremely interesting. It's extremely significant and important.

Zhao: We have wasted no time. Time is money. We have already broken a barrier between the atheists and theists. Usually there is a transparent membrane, maybe a PVC membrane, between theists and atheists. Because of that transparent membrane, the people can see each other's image but cannot feel each other's temperature. It is said that when a person gets emotional, his body temperature will go up 0.5 centigrade.

Palau: Mr. Zhao, here is a book I brought with me for you. It's called *The Creator and the Cosmos*. The author holds a PhD in astronomy and was a post-doctoral fellow at the California Institute of Technology, doing research on quasars and galaxies. I didn't write it. I wish I had but I didn't. It deals with some of the questions we've been discussing.

Zhao: I've also prepared several books. I will present them to you tomorrow. I think that book is acceptable to both theists and atheists. It's about the sites in China that have been included in the UNESCO's World Cultural Heritage List.

A street scene in Pudong

November 17, 2005,
Regal International East Asia Hotel, Shanghai

American scientists exchanging views with their Chinese counterparts on BEPC magnet

Palau: When I visited the Taoist Temple yesterday, I asked a Taoist priest about eternal life. I might ask you the same question today.

Zhao: Good. I think our dialogue is like sailing down a river. Sometimes the river goes straight and smooth, sometimes the river twists and turns. And there's beautiful landscape all along the way.

Palau: Yes. Like the Huangpu River that flows around Pudong. (*referring to the boat ride the two took together on the Huangpu in Shanghai the previous evening*).

Zhao: Maybe we can make a comparison between the Huangpu River and the Mississippi River. Both are very beautiful and neither one is jealous of the other.

Palau: Shall we continue our discussion on science and theology?

Zhao: Yes, let's continue. Theologians do their thinking in churches and they make full use of their imagination. Scientists, on the other hand, do their thinking in laboratories where, in addition to using their imagination, they must conduct experiments. For scientists, experiments and tests are essential. They have to conduct tests either in laboratories or in nature.

Even in ancient times, people had different views about the origin of knowledge. For example, according to Plato, knowledge comes from thinking, from deduction. However, his student, Aristotle, believed that knowledge is the result of the combination of thinking and reality. So the origin of knowledge has been an eternal theme for humankind since ancient times. I'm wondering in what way the theologians develop their imagination and use their brain. I'd like to seek your views. Maybe you can answer my question.

Palau: Yes. Absolutely. Faith in God encourages scientific research. It doesn't suppress it. A true knowledge of the will of God and the mind of God encourages sociological, scientific research. It actually encourages it, not suppresses it.

In the Middle Ages when the Bible was suppressed, that's when darkness came and it was called the Dark Ages. So they were afraid of scientific research. And then when there was a reformation in Europe and the discovery of the printing press, it changed the whole course of history for the last 600 years. And some of the most brilliant scientists that you mentioned yesterday, such as Newton and others, were real believers in Jesus Christ and in God. The discoverer of penicillin – his name was Fleming, a Scotsman – he was a very committed believer in the Lord and he did research based on his belief that God wanted to heal people.

Remember von Braun, the German scientist that developed the modern multi – stage rocket? He became a real believer. That shows that believing in God and knowing him doesn't in any way – I think I should emphasize this – suppress intellectual pursuits and scientific discoveries; it encourages it.

So, true Christians do not hide inside a church building. They are actually scientists, professors and research people that are involved in all areas of life, in the economy and in politics. There are people who are believers in all walks of life.

Zhao: It is recorded in the history of natural sciences, during the 17th and 18th centuries, many scientists were tortured by the Inquisition, for example, Galileo, Copernicus and also Servetus, the Spanish scientist who discovered the blood circulation system. And many important scientific discoveries met with strong opposition from the church, which demonstrated that religion posed an obstacle to science. But then, I found that some very important scientists themselves were Christians, for example, Copernicus, Galileo, Newton, Kepler and Einstein. This is something worth thinking about.

I should say in the past 100 years or so, the church, or Western religion, has greatly changed its attitude towards science. I'm
wondering how that happened and why.

Palau: Well, Galileo, also, he was persecuted. As I said
earlier, even the organized church/religion in the 17th and 18th
centuries, they were not reading the Bible. They were invent-
ing their own views about the relationship between science
and God. That's why it was called the Dark Ages. It was dark
because of the lack of biblical knowledge and many of the
religious leaders in Europe were living in total opposition to
God's rules. When your morals are down, your intellect is
darkened.

If we believe that God created the earth and all the solar
system and all the systems beyond, obviously studying it is
logical. And I think many uneducated religious leaders opposed
science because somehow they were afraid that science would
overthrow faith, but it never has. People say, "With the discoveries of science, who needs God?" But in fact, the discoveries
of science have only got to do with the present state of affairs,
with the earth and material things, and that is tremendously
valuable. Think of all the advances of science. Fantastic stuff.
We're living longer because of medical science. Although for
the moment we don't see the value of getting to the moon, one
of these days we'll realize how valuable achievements like these
are to our world.

The famous Qinciyangdian Taoist temple in Pudong, Shanghai

Zhao accompanying Palau during their visit to the
Taoist temple on Nov. 16, 2005

I remember the first Russian cosmonaut. When he went around the earth, he said, "I didn't see God anywhere." That was a pathetic statement. You don't see God in outer space. First of all, heaven is a little higher than just the space around the earth but a lot of people applauded. "Yes, see, he didn't see God." That is childish science because knowing God is a spiritual experience and it's as real as a scientific discovery that you can see in the laboratory. So it was a big mistake when they wanted science and faith in Jesus Christ to clash. You know we're friends. Friends don't clash. A person can know God personally and keep his scientific credibility a hundred percent valid.

Zhao: I believe physical existence comes first, then come activities of the human mind. In other words, matter is primary and ideas secondary, whereas for you, it's the other way around—thinking comes first, then everything else. Physicists study matter, including its structure, its motion and the interrelationship between different kinds of matter.

For example, the motion of earth and the motion of atoms, the reaction caused by a neutron hitting a nucleus of uranium, what will happen? We can see all this very clearly with instruments. You cannot measure things spiritual with any kind of instrument. People are puzzled. They don't know what a spiritual being is like. I think this may be the most difficult point to reconcile between the atheistic physicist and the theologian. As spelled out by Francis Bacon, all knowledge should be proved through experiments.

A magnetic levitation train shuttling between downtown area and Pudong International Airport in Shanghai

Palau: I think you need to distinguish between science and your commitment to atheism because you're taking a big leap between saying, "I am a scientist" and "there is no God." You cannot prove that there isn't a God. You made a decision in your head: Human creation is there and I'm going to study it, but there is no God. So you've got to keep an open mind about the existence of God. Science, you're an expert, and you can prove scientific matters. But scientists didn't believe in neutrons and so on a hundred years ago. Science has progressed. One of these days, a scientist is going to say, "I can prove that there's a God" and Dr. Zhao would say, "Hallelujah!"

Zhao: Maybe we need a really great man, one who is even greater than Albert Einstein. Since God once said that "Let there be light" and there was light, if God now says, "Let there be a scientist greater than Albert Einstein", then there will be a greater scientist.

Palau: And I've got the name of the scientist greater than Einstein—Jesus Christ.

Zhao: Yesterday you gave me a book, The Creator and the Cosmos. I think maybe the author's views overlap with yours.

Palau: You have a lot of faith, Dr. Zhao. In some ways you have more faith than I do. Here's a question. When you think of the birth of a little baby, it comes out of the mother in absolute perfection. When you think about a chick in the egg, what a strange thing, did all this happen by chance? Who taught the hen to sit on the egg? And then peck, peck, peck and here comes the little chick. Is this all by chance? And the television station can tell us tonight "Tomorrow the sun is coming out at 6:17 in the morning. On Saturday it's coming out at 6:18 in the morning. There is perfection to the cosmos. It can't be the result of a Big Bang with no God behind it. Believing that the cosmos was created by chance in a big explosion without God is like believing that the *Oxford Dictionary* was the result of an explosion in a print shop. The dictionary wasn't a result of an explosion in a print shop—some brain had to put it together—so you have more faith than I do.

Zhao: I have to admit I cannot even answer all the questions raised by myself. Actually even today, humankind is still unable to answer all the questions it has raised since ancient times. This is because the volume of the human brain is limited. The cells contained in the human brain are also limited even though they number 100 million. The human brain is like a sophisticated computer. But its power is not unlimited. For example, my brain is like a computer equipped with the 486 CPU and there are many questions it cannot answer, so I need to have a computer equipped with a higher CPU. A computer cannot reproduce another computer, but human beings can give birth to children. I think each future generation will be more intelligent than the previous one and their brains will be more and more developed. So we place high hopes on the development of science. We believe science is the number one driving force for social progress and the most

A street scene in Beijing

important productive force. The development of science has brought us closer to the truth.

Now I would like to raise a question on which you will surely have some unique views. On November 8 this year, the State Education Committee of Kansas in the United States passed a resolution to the effect that high school teachers should introduce the theory of intelligent design in their science courses. The Chinese media promptly carried the news, some covering half a page together with the opinions of the American public, both pros and cons. While I was in middle school, I attended a course on Darwin's Theory of Evolution. Darwin collected all kinds of fossils from around the world and lined up those fossils in an orderly fashion to illustrate the evolution of species. To put it simply, according to Charles Darwin, all species compete with one another and undergo natural selection. Hence, the principle of survival of the fittest and continuous adaptation and changes. Recently, 37 Nobel Prize winners made a public statement expressing opposition to introducing "intelligent design" in schools. Some scientists have said that although there are some shortcomings with the Darwinian theory, as there are some material evidence lacking in his evolution link, his views on competition among species and natural selection still stand. I'm sure among these Nobel laureates there are Christians, so it seems that there are also differences among Christians.

Palau: I want to send you a book called *Darwin's Black Box*. It's very interesting, because those missing links that you mentioned are in the area of biology, right? And there are studies now going on to show that the links are nowhere to be found. So sometimes scientists are as prejudiced at that point as ignorant religious people are. They're over-eager to demonstrate that there is no God. There is no need to be afraid that there is a creator because if there is a creator, all the findings of science will eventually come together. Many scientists are now turning from Darwin and saying, "Look, this was a hundred years ago, and the findings are still not provable today."

Now I have a question for you. Since, as a secular atheist, you don't believe in God, how did the world come to be? How does an atheist explain the existence of the cosmos?

Zhao: Theologians say, "God created the cosmos." It's a very clever answer. It's also a once-and-for-all way to answer the question. I think this is just one of the possible answers humans can offer. But I cannot answer it by saying, "I don't know, but God knows." I believe those questions that I can't answer now, our future generations may be able to answer, step by step, hundreds or thousands of years from now. Now, maybe I can also raise a question that you may not be able to answer right away. If there is a God, who created him?

Palau: I knew you'd ask me that. And I have no idea. When we get to heaven, we'll find out because it says in the Bible, "We will know as we are known." So if you come with me to heaven when we both die, we'll talk about it in heaven, is that fair?

Zhao: If heaven really exists, I wonder whether our images will change. Would we still be able to recognize each other?

Palau: Absolutely. If we can recognize each other in China, and we'll be much brighter in heaven, we'll recognize each other. I'll come looking for you.

Zhao: Should we have a code so we'd recognize each other?

Palau: I'll give you my card.

Zhao: In case our images have changed by then, I will say "Mississippi River," and you'll say "Yangtze River," and click! We'd recognize each other.

Palau: Good idea!

Zhao: A beautiful story, born of our common imagination.

PART
SEVEN

On Religion and Social Harmony

A night scene of Potala Palace

World Buddhism Forum held in Hangzhou, Zhejiang Province

Zhao Qizheng saluting the Egyptian soldiers in front of the Pyramid on Aug. 7, 2005

Palau: As a believer in Jesus Christ, I feel religion is closely related to society and our daily life. For example, Christ has a direct bearing on social stability because a true Christian will respect those in authority. Christ has much impact on intellectual pursuit and eternal life. Christ provides answers to such questions as "Who am I?" "Where do I come from?" Why am I here?" "Where am I heading?" and "What is the aim of my existence?" Christ has an impact on our psychological balance, family harmony, social ethics and the elimination of crime and evil. Christ is also concerned with the society and its economy. "Those who do not work, do not eat." This is a principle which can propel people to work hard because God respects and appreciates honest and trustworthy people.

Zhao: Religion, as a cultural system of long-standing, has had a widespread impact on the political, economic and cultural life of society. This is true not only with regard to Christianity, but also with regard to Buddhism, Taoism, Islam and other reli-

The Dead Sea Scrolls

gions. The ethical teachings inherent in religion, urging people to do away with evil and upholding righteousness, play a positive role in encouraging the believers to pursue a moral life. Religion also plays a positive role in providing psychological comfort to the believers, pacifying their emotions and adjusting their feelings. It has had a far-reaching influence on architecture, painting, sculpture, music, literature and philosophy. *The Dead Sea Scrolls* which were discovered between the 1940s and 60s left a deep impression on me when I visited Israel this year because they provided a convincing record of the religious culture of the Hebrew people. The Pyramids of Egypt, the Cathedral of Notre Dame de Paris and the Buddhist temples that are ubiquitous in China represent the quintessence of architectural art. The Mogao Grottoes of Dunhuang in Northwest China embrace the best of Chinese, Indian, Greek and Islamic cultures. Many exquisite ancient murals and sculptures have left us with an accretion of brilliant cultures in the long span of history. Religions have had a great influence on the development of music too, as testified

A figure of Buddha in Mogao Grottos, Dunhuang

Murals of flying Aparas

by Handel's *Messiah*, Haydn's *Creation*, Beethoven's *Solemn Messiah* and the Buddhist and Taoist music in China.

I think there are many similarities between Christian ethics and Chinese ethics. According to the Bible, there is a Golden Rule, which says, "Do unto others what you would others do to you." In China, there are these words by Confucius, "Do not do to others what you would not want others to do to you." I think the core meaning of those two sayings is the same, but formulated from different perspectives.

Palau: Both sides of the same coin.

Ye Xiaowen, Director of China National Bureau on Religious Affairs, and U.S. President Jimmy Carter at the Exhibition Tour of *China Church Bible Affairs* to the United States in July, 2006

Director Ye Xiaowen meeting with Cardinal Edgar McCarrick, archbishop of Washington, on July 29, 2003

Zhao: So your comments about ethics are very easy to understand. The essence of Confucian ethics is that people should love one another. Confucius regarded that as the highest realm of ethics, which includes how you correctly treat your sovereign, your parents, your brothers and your friends. I think both Confucian ethics and Christian ethics have played a positive role in promoting harmony in the family, the cell of society. I think a good example of this is after the 9.11 incident, the American society, which is mainly Christian, demonstrated great unity and determination to resist terrorism.

Not long before the 9.11 incident, Rupert Murdoch, Chairman of News Corporation, invited me to a banquet at the World Trade Center. Soon after I returned to China, the Twin Towers were destroyed. I was deeply shocked.

After 9.11, I visited the United States again. I went to the churches and saw many people mourning the dead. I saw the items left by those who perished—their photos, their hats, their clothes, their postcards... I could feel the love and the feeling of loss by the whole society.

So I should say that Christian ethics have made a positive contribution to family and social harmony. Although I was a foreigner and non-Christian, I shared the same feelings, same emotion, as the Americans and the Christians.

But history has shown that there are also some negative effects of religion. Religion has its historical and national background. Rational theists and atheists should see not only the positive side of religion but also the limitations of each religion. Some of its negative effects are reflected mainly in its failure to exert the same kind of influence it exerts within its own religion and sects on relations between different religions and sects, different ethnic groups and different countries.

In the summer of this year, I visited Israel and Egypt. I went to the famous Wailing Wall. I found many Jewish people standing reverently there. But I felt uneasy because this was a place of conflicts, political conflicts and also religious conflicts. In Egypt, the Egyptian government sent four bodyguards to protect me. They followed us around in a mini-van. But this only made me feel even more uneasy. I think the reason the different religions cannot coexist in harmony is because each thinks it is the greatest

Jerusalem, holy city of the world's three major religions

The Wailing Wall of Jerusalem

religion and its god is the only God. No one is willing to give way, so there can be no reconciliation. However, Buddhism is an exception. It is tolerant towards other religions. I think the various religions should be tolerant toward one another and respect one another. Only then can there be harmony among them. So my assessment is: Religion may play a positive role of enhancing harmony within its own religion and country, but in the world at large, sometimes it may play a negative role in relations among different religions and nations. I wonder whether you agree with my view.

Palau: You've got a lot of basic points. But I think you were talking about four issues here today: religion, evil, war and a harmonious society. Religion is man's effort to find God. Christianity does not call itself a religion. True Christianity is a relationship, a personal relationship with God himself. Really, a true Christian presents Jesus Christ as the way, and it offers that way to everybody around the world. But it doesn't force a person. You are free to say "no". And if you say "no," you are on your own. But I still love you and respect you. We are still friends. But men have created a whole machinery around Jesus Christ and the Bible. It's like you and I can be friends—we are friends now—but some people could start building a whole machinery around us. For instance, some people suggested, "Before you can meet with Mr. Zhao the next time you go to China, you have to do all these things: You must bring a picture of Mr. Zhao and you must burn a candle in front of him, or his picture, because he's a very important official in China. You must walk on your knees all the way from the door to Mr. Zhao. And then when you get there, you kiss his hand and then you take three steps backward. Here we're friends and somebody created a religion between us. I would say to that person, "Forget it. I've got Mr. Zhao's telephone. I'm going to call him directly. Forget all this candle and photographs and walking on your knees. We have a relationship."

Religion has not caused all the wars. World War I, World War II, and the Vietnam War had nothing to do with religion. Hitler was an atheist. He got the war going. Religion causes troubles sometimes, but Jesus? No. The troubles you saw between Israel and the surrounding nations aren't really religious. Religion is used as a tool. It's territorial, it's economic, and to stir up the people, they wave the flag of religion.

So it comes back to greed and evil. These people use religion as a banner but they can also use atheism. And the problem with war is that we are a fallen race—that's the problem. Science is neutral. You can use it to heal cancer patients or you can develop a bomb to drop on Hiroshima and blow it away. In fact, technology and science have made wars even more dangerous. We don't give up science because of the atomic bomb or the hydrogen bomb. That's a misuse of science.

So evil is in the heart. The problem is not science and definitely not Christianity. It is the human heart that needs to be changed. The heart is evil. We have wrong inclinations. We are greedy.

I see millions of Chinese turning their hearts over to Jesus. It has been happening in the last few years. Every generation needs to have a change of heart because a harmonious society cannot come if my heart is evil and your heart is evil and we're clashing with each other. That's why it says in the Bible, "If anyone is in Christ, you become a new person. The old has passed away and everything becomes new." It's a spiritual scientific experiment.

When I was a university student, that's what convinced me about following Jesus – that you see change in people's lives for the good when they truly surrender their hearts and live out their faith following Jesus. There's a change. And this spreads harmony because you love your neighbor as yourself. I've come to love you, to respect you, and the fact that you say "I'm an atheist" doesn't bother me, except that I'm praying one day Mr. Zhao is going to give his life to Jesus and we'll be brothers. And I can see you as a scientist spreading peace all over the world. But that's the effect of following Jesus. That's why it has an im-

Zhao Qizheng with performers of Tibetan Children's Art Troupe retuning from a tour abroad on Oct. 9, 1999

pact, as you said, on certain cultures, and it's having an impact, I think, in China. It's going to be beautiful in the next century. So many bright young Chinese are taking Jesus seriously and the Bible seriously. I notice that. So I think the revolution of 1949 has sort of cleared the mind in China and it's ready for a spiritual awakening. That's the way I interpret the history of China in the last 50 years.

Zhao: I think I can endorse many of the words you have just said. The founding of the PRC in 1949 cleared up not only those bad things in society but also people's soul. But I think this is a process. It's not something that happens overnight. Because now that the people have found the mode and road of development best suited to them, they are more spirited and energetic. Today, what China produces in a single day is tantamount to a month's production in the 1940s. And that's not only because of the progress made in science and technology, but also because the Chinese people's mind has been emancipated.

What you said just now about the Christian spirit has enhanced my knowledge of Christianity. I fully agree with you that there are people who wave the flag of religion out of greed and evil. These should not be confused with religion. For instance, a cult is, in essence, not a religion, but an evil organization. It is a pity that some people, ignorant of the facts, have been misled and have been exploited by the cult organizers.

Palau: Now I have two things I want to say. One, I read in the paper that the Chinese are the most contented people, right now, of any nation in the world. So there's been tremendous progress materially, economically, and scientifically. China is moving forward fast. Seventy-six percent of the Chinese say they're very contented, with great hope that the future is getting better. Two, in terms of the number of religious people in China, the optimists say that there's a hundred million. That's why in the United States and in England, there's great excitement about China.

About 20 years ago, I was having a festival in Hong Kong before I came over to the mainland of China and in the stadium I said, "China is going to be the great powerhouse a hundred years from now."

I have a song in my briefcase called *I Love China*. I heard a children's choir singing it in Beijing a year ago. There was one child from every province of China and when they sang this song, there was a big screen; it had views of various provinces of China and they put on the screen the translation in English of the words. I just sat there and cried like a baby. Even thinking about it now, I almost cry. And I'm not a crybaby.

My mother taught me to love China. When I was a little boy, we used to pray for China all the time. And to see China flourishing, it's amazing. And as a Christian, I think if the foundation of Jesus builds it up, it's going to be even more amazing.

Zhao: I am deeply moved by your love for China and your wish for China to develop further and for the Chinese people to live a happy life. China's development is the result of putting into practice the theory of building socialism with Chinese characteristics. And that is built on the basis of the country's own cultural tradition. It is hard to imagine that it could be built on the basis of imported culture. Just now you said that you could be good friends with atheists. I agree to that. I had the same feeling when we were singing the song *Auld Lang Syne* together. That Scottish folk song became very popular in China after it was introduced into this country as the theme song of the American film "*Waterloo Bridge*".

So maybe I can summarize your remarks and my remarks into the following points: The differences between atheism and theism do not constitute an obstacle to our friendship. The common objective of the theists and atheists is to promote global harmony.

Times Square in New York (right)

A street scene in Chicago

A Washington, D.C., post office just before Christmas

A movie poster for the film *Waterloo Bridge*

Palau: Yes.

Zhao: Mutual understanding and frequent exchanges of views are essential and effective.

Palau: Yes.

Zhao: We are against greed, we are against selfishness, we are against laziness, and we are against evil and wars. In ancient history, there were frequent religious wars. You explained that religion is not the cause of all wars. The fundamental cause is man's greed and evil. I would further hope that religion and religious sects would play a role in preventing wars and not be exploited by warmongers and militarists.

Palau: That's true.

Zhao: You said that Adolf Hitler was an atheist. We also know that he was not only a war maniac, but also an extreme anti-Semitist. Hitler capitalized on the religious prejudices prevalent at the time to serve his own political ambitions.

Palau: There's so much that we have in common. From my perspective, my dream would be that every Chinese person

Palau directing a small band welcoming him in front of the
Shanghai Oriental Pearl TV Tower in Nov. 2005

would find peace with God through Jesus. That's my dream.
Because we all know we're going to die and the interesting
thing is that Jesus offers the absolute assurance of eternal life
to every sinner who repents and believes in him. He doesn't
expect us to be perfect, otherwise nobody would have eternal
life. He offers us forgiveness and then the assurance of heaven
forever when we die.

I particularly love this verse from the Gospel of John. "The
Son of God did not come into the world to condemn the world
but that through him the world would be saved."

Zhao: I, too, have a dream. My dream is that the exchanges
between religious believers and non-believers will become an
important part of contemporary culture. The United States and

China are both great nations. The United States is the largest developed country in the world and China is the largest developing country in the world. We should make more active and effective efforts to promote the exchanges between the Chinese and American peoples. Using IT jargon, I think there should be several friendly "interfaces" between China and the United States. China-US dialogue should be comprehensive and not limited to the Chinese Foreign Ministry and the US State Department. It should include religious dialogue and dialogue between the religious and non-religious people.

Palau: Yes.

Zhao: Someone once said, "In much wisdom is much vexation." The more intelligent, the more concerns. But I don't think that's true. You're very intelligent but you are still very optimistic.

Palau: Today I was thinking that friends should be honest with each other and sometimes it hurts a little when friends tell the truth to each other. But it's always for good. And I was reminded of the words of King Solomon, the wisest man in the world. You quoted the Book of Proverbs yesterday—Solomon wrote it—and I was reminded this morning of these words of his: "Better are the wounds of a friend than the kisses of an enemy." The wounds may hurt a little but it heals afterwards. So that's a good concept, isn't it?

Zhao: I'd like to echo your viewpoints with a very popular

Chinese saying, "The medicine may taste bitter, but is good for your health. Good advice may sound repugnant to the ear, but is good for your conduct." I think the two sayings are essentially the same. I mentioned earlier that Confucius had said, "At 60, my ears are open to harsh words." That is a sign of self-cultivation and maturity.

Palau: Now, at what age should a person give his heart to Jesus Christ? The younger the better?

Zhao: Maybe influenced by their families, some people become Christians when they are still very young. But for most Chinese families, they are not Christian. Young people are mainly influenced by family, school and society.

Friends from European countries and the United States have asked me: What kind of a society is China trying to build? The Chinese people are building a socialist society with Chinese characteristics, a harmonious society. That is now our national policy. This harmonious society certainly includes harmony within a religion and among different religions, as well as between religious circles and non-religious circles. The various religions in China all help to promote harmony in the course of social development.

Palau: Well, I will try in my little way to create all the harmony possible between our two countries. And in China, encourage all the young followers of Jesus to love one another, to really respect one another. So that'll be my little contribution.

Zhao: Since Sino-US relations are most important for both countries, I think your contribution will not be a little one, but a very big one. I would like to express my respect not only to you, but also to all our friends who have contributed to Sino-US friendship.

Palau: After my trip to Beijing last May, I was talking on American TV about a bookstore I visited that sells Bibles and all the religious books, but people said, "No, it can't be." They still have this notion. They're behind the times on information about China.

I told them I was in the printing shop of the Amity Foundation in Nanjing which is managed by a New Zealander and they put out millions of Bibles all over China. And they showed me a map of China with all the distribution centers and I asked the manager, "How do you distribute the Bible all over China?" And he said, "The China Post."

Zhao: I think most Americans know less about China than Chinese know about the United States. A few years ago, a New York ballet troupe came to Beijing. When they were making hotel reservations, they said they must be hotels with bathrooms. Also, several years ago, when the president of a radio station based in Washington visited China, he brought with him a lot of bread and cookies because some people had told him there might be some problem with the food in China.

Palau: The change in China has been so accelerated, the

news takes a while to get back to Americans and memories of the Cold War are still in the air.

Zhao: I once talked with Dr. Kissinger about this issue and I told him I think there are two areas of misunderstanding among Americans about China. One is that China's foreign policy is identical with that of the former Soviet Union, and two, after quick economic development, China will become a source of economic friction and competition for the United States, just like Japan was in the 1970s.

Palau: Economic competition is bound to happen. You've got four times the population of America. And if America doesn't keep up its educational system at top flight, China is going to win.

History shows that when a country or an empire becomes rich, it becomes passive. It begins to just want to live off the past, and they miss out on the present and the future. History goes in a cycle. When a nation becomes rich and there's so much abundance, there is also a great potential for it to become corrupt in the moral sense and decay begins.

As for the first misunderstanding, that China is like the Soviet Union, I think that's the biggest misunderstanding. Do you agree?

Zhao: Dr. Kissinger said that since Americans are very pragmatic, they attach great importance to economic competition, whereas a much smaller percentage of people may regard China as being like the former Soviet union, politically speaking. So

Beijing: antiquity and modernity coexisting harmoniously

your view matches that of Dr. Kissinger. Maybe you can become the Secretary of State for the United States.

Palau: Oh, thank you. No, thank you.

Zhao: Dr. Kissinger could not become the US President since he was born in Germany. I'm wondering whether you were born in the United States or in Argentina? Would you go into politics?

Palau: I was born in Argentina. I don't have a chance.

Zhao: But I know you can influence the president. I think there's a big difference between China and the former Soviet Union. When a theory is introduced into China, there will be a process of localization or "China-ization". We would have to adapt it to the actual conditions in China. So, for example, China's market economy is different from that in the United States, in the European countries. But even in Europe, the French market economy is different from the British and German market economies. And in Asia, the market economy in Japan differs from that in other East Asian countries. There are many suggestions for China's market economy. We listen carefully to their suggestions. We will accept those which suit the current Chinese situation.

In China, different cities and regions have different blue-prints for economic development. The successful experience of one region may not be good for another region. In the world, there is no universal model of a market economy, and less still, a universally applicable political mode.

At a Fashion competition

Foreigners' Street in Dali, Yunnan Province

Beijing International Civilians Sports and Culture Get-together held in the Juyong Pass of the Great Wall

Fashionable with a section of a Buddhist scripture printed on his T-shirt

Beijing Houhai (Rear Sea) Alley Tour

A street scene in Beijing with a poster for a harmonious society

It's the Neighborhood Festival! People are greeting one another with flowers

Palau: That's a big discussion. Solomon said, "Of the making of books, there is no end." So we have to put limits on our knowledge.

Zhao: How many books have you already published?

Palau: Oh, I think 48. And how many have you published?

Zhao: I've published just a few, since in China a civil servant has little time to write books. This book, *Introducing China to the World*, was published in May this year. It contains twenty of my speeches and forty dialogues with foreigners. Since then, the book has been re-printed four times. The publisher is pleased and they would like to publish a sequel to it.

Palau: Your book basically deals with understanding cultures of other countries and international understanding.

Zhao: Exactly. In this book, you can find my dialogues with political figures or media people from Germany, France, the United Kingdom, the United States, South Korea and Japan. There are others not yet published. For the second volume of this book, the publisher plans to include the transcript of our first dialogue in May this year. What do you think?

Palau: Oh, I would be honored if you'd do that.

Zhao: Previously, it was carried in a magazine and some of the readers thought of you as a man of great wisdom and a very friendly person. Actually, I, too, benefited from the radiance of your wisdom.

Palau: Now you sound like a poet!

Zhao: I have more respect for a philosopher, and you're a philosopher. A poet has strong emotions, but doesn't have to have strong logic. A professor of communications and media at Tsinghua University said that after reading the transcripts of our dialogues, he was at a loss for words, as all comments seemed unnecessary.

Palau: Mr. Zhao, there seems to be a love affair between China and me. I've always loved China; now China loves me.

Zhao: Well, actually I liked you. Now, I love you. Yesterday, when we sang the song together....

Palau: *Auld Lang Syne*?

Zhao: Yes, together in front of the orchestra at the entrance of the Oriental Pearl TV Tower, I had this feeling of closeness. I think of all the people present, we two were the oldest. They are all young and full of pep, but you know what? Older people have more to reflect on.

Palau: That's right. Now I have another point that I wanted to make. Is there any chance that when we publish the English edition in America, could I invite you to visit the United States? And when you come, I think we could have you interviewed by *The Washington Post* and *The New York Times* and *The Los Angeles Times* and other papers and television. It would help in the whole dialogue of respect between the United States and China. It really would help a lot because you represent China honorably, clearly and truthfully, so it's very good.

Launching of the new book *Introducing China to the World—Mr. Zhao Qizheng's Speeches and Dialogues*

Zhao: Finally, I think we should thank the China Association of International Friendly Contact for helping to make our dialogues possible. We have cooperated very well. In China, we have a saying, "After crossing the river, we should not tear down the bridge."

A street scene in Beijing on Christmas Eve

Palau: We have spent two days together.

Zhao: If we had the time, we could continue our dialogue for another 20 days.

ABOUT THE AUTHORS

LUIS PALAU was born in the province of Buenos Aires, Argentina, in 1934.

He attended Saint Alban's College, a British boarding school in Argentina, part of the Cambridge University Overseas Program. In 1961, he completed the Graduate Program, Multnomah School of the Bible (now Multnomah Biblical Seminary, Portland, Oregon).

Among the honors he received are honorary doctorate of divinity degrees from Talbot Theological Seminary in La Mirada, California; Wheaton College in Illinois; and George Fox College in Newberg, Oregon as well as honorary doctorate of theology degree from Mariano Galvez University in Guatemala City.

Mr. Palau committed his life to Jesus Christ at age 12. At age 18, he began preaching on weekends while working at an Argentine bank. By 1957, he and several other young men organized a tent evangelism and radio ministry in Argentina.

Mr. Palau has published 45 books and booklets in English and Spanish, including *High Definition Life* (Revell Publishing, a division of Baker Publishing, 2005), *It's a God Thing* (Doubleday, 2001), *Where Is God When Bad Things Happen?* (Doubleday, 1999), *God Is Relevant* (Doubleday, 1997) and *The Only Hope for America* (Crossway Books, 1996).

ZHAO QIZHENG was born in Beijing in 1940. He graduated in 1963 from the University of Science and Technology of China, majoring in experimental nuclear physics. He was then engaged in scientific research until 1984 and still holds three patents of invention. From 1984, he served as Vice Mayor of Shanghai, Director-general of the Management Committee of Shanghai Pudong New Area, and Minister of the State Council Information Office in China. He is now Vice Chairman of the Foreign Affairs Committee of the Chinese People's Political Consultative Conference and dean of the School of Journalism and Communication, Renmin University of China.

Mr. Zhao's publications include *Introducing China to the World: Zhao Qizheng and the Art of Communication* (New World Press, 2006), *America and Americans through Chinese Eyes* (China Intercontinental Press, 2005), *Introducing China to the World: Zhao Qizheng's Speeches and Dialogues* (New World Press, 2005) and *New Century · New Pudong* (Fudan University Press, 1994).